In a world filled with relationship and self-help books, *Tune into Love* is a rare find. Through her years of expertise as a therapist and life coach, Margaret A. McCraw has compiled a refreshing and comprehensive guide book to help you master your relationships and your life. *Tune Into Love* is a veritable one-stop shop for learning the application of proactive ideas that simply can not be found elsewhere. This book is a shining gem, a tool you can use daily to repattern your thinking processes and Margaret McCraw's writing is sterling! Margaret teaches us how relationships do not need to be a downward spiral of repeating disappointments but that we can truly learn to live from glory to glory. Well done!

—Amelia Kinkade, author of *Straight from the Horse's Mouth*

There are surprisingly few people who truly understand how to take control of their lives and manifest their envisioned destinies. There are even fewer who have successfully taught others to do this. Margaret McCraw is one of these rare individuals. *Tune into Love* is not just a book you should read; it is a book you should savor and digest and then allow to permeate to the very core of your being.

—Morton C. Orman, M.D., author of *The 14 Day Stress Cure*

Margaret McCraw's *Tune into Love* is a spiritual compass for finding clarity of direction in one's relationships. It is a book that overflows with a wealth of transformative personal development techniques that help readers attract their ideal partner while discovering their own unique sacred lifewalk.

—Jayne Howard Feldman, author of *Commune with the Angels*

Tune into Love is the right medicine for discovering the strength that is within each one of us. Margaret McCraw has provided us with a compass which will lead us to inner piece, spiritual and mental well being, and the partner we've always wanted and thought existed only in fantasies. This is a compelling book-a must read for all which provides the key ingredients for realizing our full potential and creating a life time of bliss.

—Oscar Morgan, Chief Operating Officer, National Mental Health Association

Tune into Love is a complete step by step guide to show you how to attract and create the perfect relationship for you. Margaret takes us on a journey of self discovery and inspires us to be the star of our life and achieve our dreams. A penetrating, practical book for those who aspire to greatness.

—Brendan Nichols, author of *Your Soul Purpose*

In *Tune into Love* Margaret McCraw taps into spiritual wisdom, combined with sound psychological principles, to teach us how to manifest the partner we've always wanted. It is refreshing to see such clear thinking. This book is a rare find.

—Reverend James L. Lockard,
Pastor of Religious Science Fort Lauderdale
and author of *Survival Thinking*

Margaret McCraw has combined her thorough understanding of psychology with her deep knowledge of spiritual wisdom, to create a book that will inspire you to attract your ideal partner. The principles put forth are profound and the exercises will boost your attraction power. If you desire to be a winner in your own life, this is the book for you!

—Rev. Eva Gabrielle, Unity Minister in Baltimore, MD

Tune into Love is an internal optometrist! A wonderful guide to help you identify and create a divine relationship. Even more importantly, it is a torch that will make your heart and soul ecstatically happy.

—Hope Karan Gerecht, author of *Healing Design:
Practical Feng Shui for Healthy and Gracious Living*

Margaret McCraw's book, *Tune into Love*, empowers everyone to overcome limiting belief systems and develop new thought processes to create purposeful and passionate intimate relationships. A powerful tool to read, utilize, and find answers to our desires for happiness. Just superb!

—Allyson Walsh, author of *The Sacred Tarot Unveiled*

Margaret McCraw's book *Tune into Love* is a lighthearted and passionate guide to using universal principles to attract the kind of life partner you have always longed for. True love exists—and this book will help you realize the truest desires of your heart.

—Jeffrey Proctor, Pastor of Religious Science, Baltimore, MD

Tune Into Love

Attract Romance Through the Power of Vibrational Matching

Margaret McCraw, Ph.D.

Cover design by Tiffany McCord
Cover digital imagery © 2004 GettyImages/
PhotoDisc/John Slater. All rights reserved.

Hampton Roads Publishing Company, Inc.
1125 Stoney Ridge Road
Charlottesville, VA 22902

434-296-2772
fax: 434-296-5096
e-mail: hrpc@hrpub.com
www.hrpub.com

If you are unable to order this book from your local
bookseller, you may order directly from the publisher.
Call 1-800-766-8009, toll-free.

Library of Congress Cataloging-in-Publication Data

McCraw, Margaret.
  Tune into love : attract romance through the power of vibrational
matching / Margaret McCraw.
      p. cm.
  Summary: "A therapist introduces Vibrational Matching, a
process for attracting the right person at the right time in your
life"--Provided by publisher.
  Includes bibliographical references.
  ISBN 1-57174-430-4 (5-1/2x8-1/2 tp : alk. paper)
  1. Man-woman relationships. 2. Love. I. Title.
HQ801.M4872 2005
306.7--dc22
                                          200500571

              10 9 8 7 6 5 4 3 2 1

    Printed on acid-free paper in Canada

This book is dedicated to my dear mother, Ethel Lucille Sumner, who has inspired and co-created this book. I am eternally grateful for her loving and thoughtful guidance, as well as her joyous presence in my life. She has my heart and my soul, forever.

Table of Contents

Part One: Create through Consciousness

Part Two: Becoming a Vibrational
Match to Your Desires

Part Three: Frequently Asked Questions

Acknowledgments

First and foremost, I am eternally grateful to Jerry and Esther Hicks and the family of Abraham. Your teachings on vibrational alignment are a great gift to the world and to me personally, and have heavily influenced the content of this book. Words cannot adequately express my love and deep appreciation for your willingness to come forward with your guidance.

I am very grateful to Robert Friedman and the staff of Hampton Roads Publishing, for their commitment to offering books that are uplifting to the human spirit. Their work is a guiding light to the world. I thank them for believing in me, and for all of their effort in bringing this book to fruition.

I am very appreciative of Alan Cohen, who has offered his friendship, love, and light on a number of occasions, including finalizing the title of this book. He is a dear soul and I am grateful for his presence in my life.

I also want to extend heartfelt thanks to Joelle Delbourgo for offering her insights and support for this book. Her integrity is something to be admired.

To the great teachers who have influenced this work: Dr. Carl Gustav Jung, whose guiding light has enveloped me and taught me the truth of who I am. Thank you for your constant love and support. Masters James and Barnabus, who continuously offer me hope and inspiration. The light of your consciousness lives on forever.

Many special friends offered suggestions for this book, including editorial advice—some I want to mention by name: Ellen Savarese, Ron Olson, Tom Kapp, Jon Riggle, Eileen Hansen, Joan Duhaime, Bob Olson, Scott Warehime, Clair Gerus, Allyson Walsh, Mona McLaughlin, Barbara Mallery, and Jill Adler. I thank you with all my heart.

I gratefully acknowledge J. R. Oyler, who offered his loving assistance on numerous occasions during the proposal stage of this project. I can't thank him enough for his tireless effort in seeing me through many late nights preparing for this day. He is a gift to the Universe!

My appreciation is also extended to Rosie Howard, who lovingly assisted with formatting and preparing this manuscript for the publisher, and to Bill Marchiony, who lovingly offered his screensaver quotes.

The consciousness of many individuals has heavily influenced me and this work. First, I would like to thank my mother, Ethel Lucille Sumner, for teaching me that the Universe is abundant and limitless, for constantly reinforcing that I can have whatever I desire, and for co-creating this book. You are near and dear to me. In addition, I would like to thank my father, Arthur Clayton, whose presence has taught me the strength of my spirit; my Aunt Ila, who showed me, by example, the power of being fearless; my Aunt Alma, who reminded me to take time to enjoy the flowers; my Aunt Vera, whose sweetness fills my soul with beautiful memories; my grandmother, Mary Ann Gennettie Ellen Sumner, whose constant love reminds me that I am One with the Universe; my grandfather, Martin David Sumner, whose beautiful independent spirit and strong sense of integrity leave a lasting impression; Helen Pyecha for showing me how to live optimistically every moment of every day, regard-

Acknowledgments

less of what is before you; Althea Hallock, who demonstrated appreciation and enthusiasm for all my endeavors; Bob Cartwright and Olga and Ambrose Worrall, who opened a door through which I continue to walk, on deeper and deeper levels; Sr. Suzanne Marie Foley, who gave me a deeper understanding of the meaning of determination and perseverance; Dr. Art Wagner, who showed me that our eyes are the window to our soul; Dr. Blackstone, Dr. Albertson, and Dr. Tom and Marilyn Cimonetti, who reinforce my sense of well-being; my Lakota friends, Silver Moon and Silver Arrow, who guide and inspire me to greater heights.

Finally, I am thankful to my circle of family and friends, especially my sister, Shirley Jean Garlan, who inspired me with her thoughtful messages of love and support and an occasional verse of "Zippity Doo Dah." In addition, I feel much appreciation to Ken and Carole McCraw, who offered loving encouragement; Mary and Bob Borst, for their support and thoughtful suggestions on some of the diagrams; David and Marshall McCraw for their encouragement and suggestions for this book; and Dorothy Walton and Ruby and Dean Larrowe for their constant love. Much love and gratitude is extended to Nathaniel and Phillip for their inspiration, enthusiasm for life, and for demonstrating pure love and joy every moment of each perfect day. Special thanks and love to Ron Olson for his encouragement, willingness to be available day and night, and thoughtful suggestions for this book.

All of you light up my life. I love you so much.

Author's Note

Case examples presented in this book are composites of individual situations; some are fictionalized to better demonstrate a point or to obscure individual identities. Similarities between these anecdotes and the experiences of actual persons are coincidental.

The examples in this book are applicable to any relationship regardless of personal preferences.

I define Vibrational Matching as "the deliberate intention to energize our desires by vibrating at a level equal to them." Vibrational Matching can be used to attract *anything* we want; however, for the purpose of this book, the desire is *always* defined as a romantic relationship. This term stems from the work of Abraham-Hicks, who teaches vibrational alignment and how to be a vibrational match to your desires (see acknowledgments and introduction to this book).

Vibrational Counselors, referenced throughout this book, were fictionalized to demonstrate a point for teaching purposes. However, certification for psychotherapists, life coaches, and other healthcare professionals in Vibrational Techniques is being offered through The Institute of Vibrational Synchronicity. This institute has recently been established by Margaret McCraw in conjunction with the publishing and launching of this book. Counselors, therapists, and other healthcare professionals are trained in vibrational techniques that are integrated with clinical as well as other therapeutic modalities. See the back of this book for training, certification, and counseling services.

The phrase "highest good" is used throughout this book. It is not intended to convey a religious connotation. The reader is welcome to substitute the term "best interest" if he or she is more comfortable with that.

Finally, the word Universe is capitalized throughout the book. I define the Universe as more than space. It is the pure source of all energy—infinite intelligence. I believe this energy source is part of everything in the cosmos, is available to all of us, and that we are all interconnected. Please feel free to substitute Universe with your choice of word for a higher power.

Foreword

The world is changing rapidly, and many of us are trying our best to keep up with it. Many of the models of success and tools for achievement that our parents and teachers offered us don't quite fit into the world as we know it. Anything that brings us closer to inner peace is more valuable than ever.

At this time in our personal and planetary evolution, we need bridge builders. People who can bridge the world we were born into, with the world we are living in, to the world we would create. People who can bridge professional growth and inner contentment. People who can bridge spiritual values and material life. People who can reconnect us with the selves from which we have become disconnected.

Margaret McCraw is such a bridge builder. She has a unique and gifted ability to marry lofty principles with practical application. She is a therapist and a real person. She is willing to expose her personal challenges in the service of illuminating the lessons she has learned. She knows the corporate world, as well as the hearts of those who may not know their own. She lives in the real world, while holding a vision of a better life and stepping toward it.

Tune into Love is one of the most grounded, practical, and penetrating guidebooks to personal development I have seen. Here Margaret will walk you, step by step, through exercises that will help you discover your own truth and then put it into action in ways that get results, the relationship you've always desired. With so many theoretical books in the marketplace, it is a pleasure to find one that empowers the reader to find his own answers. And that is the way it should be.

I promise you that if you do the processes in this book, your life will change in a huge way, and the relationship you've dreamed about will come to fruition. Here Margaret McCraw shows you how to use your mind in ways that will get you what you want, rather than what you fear. These techniques of deliberate creation are unsurpassed. They work because they are founded on universal principles that come to life as you apply them. And what better healing tools than self-belief and forgiveness? All of therapy can be boiled down to these two golden elements.

You are about to undertake a great adventure—unearthing the jewels of wisdom that live inside you, and then bringing them forth in splendor; rediscovering the power that you have given away, but are now ready to reclaim. Along your way your greatest asset is honesty. Simply tell the truth about what you feel and what you want. Trust that you are worthy of the good you desire. Rewarding relationships, prosperity, good health, and inner peace are not too much to ask; anything else is too little.

Enjoy your journey.

Alan Cohen

Preface

A few months ago I was listening to the radio while driving from Baltimore to Virginia, and I heard a radio talk-show host interview a relationship "expert" on the subject of attracting romance. Her advice was directed toward women and included the following: 1) wear sensual clothing all of the time, because you never know when you will bump into "Mr. Right"; 2) go out to social events or bars or clubs at least four times per week, and make it your goal to give your telephone number to at least three single men during each outing; 3) lower your standards, because this will allow more potential dates to be available to you; and 4) put your career and related goals on hold until you have achieved your relationship dream, because competition is great, and time is of the essence.

I could hardly believe what I was hearing. I thought: Do people really believe this? The young, single female anchor protested a bit, because she felt that following these recommendations would deplete her energy. She also hesitated at the thought of lowering her standards, exclaiming, "What's the point of attracting someone I don't want?" Her counterpart at the radio station told her she was resisting good advice, and he thought she should pay attention if she ever wanted to get married. As I listened to the dialogue, I could hardly restrain myself from calling the station and responding to the advice being given. Driving prohibited me from doing so.

Had I called the station, I would have told the female anchor that the guest speaker's recommendations were based on fear and scarcity. These suggestions would, in fact, keep someone from attracting a desirable relationship. I wanted to explain to her that chasing after something ensures that it will remain beyond our reach. I wanted her to know that lowering our standards creates unhappy relationships and a strong market for divorce attorneys. I so much wanted her to understand that putting one's happiness or peace of mind on hold, while waiting for a desire to come to fruition, creates a lifetime of unfulfilled dreams. I wanted to explain three simple truths:

1. You can have it all.
2. There is an abundance of desirable relationships, easily available to each one of us.
3. Love is a state of mind that is fostered and re-created when you truly love yourself.

As the radio show ended I continued my commute, feeling passion and purpose running through my veins. I never contacted the radio station to offer my unsolicited advice, but I did go home and begin writing this book. It is offered to you with love and light.

Introduction

The basis of life is absolute freedom,
The objective of life is absolute joy,
The result of life is absolute growth.
—Abraham-Hicks

During the past decade I have embarked upon an intense and delightful study of the Science of Deliberate Creation and the Art of Allowing. These teachings are inspired guidance, brought forth from the family of Abraham, and delivered through Jerry and Esther Hicks, authors of *Ask and It Is Given*. Their message focuses on acknowledging our well-being and aligning our vibration to become a match for our desires.

Abraham's work has inspired many great teachers, some of which include Wayne Dyer, Alan Cohen, Louise Hay, Neale Donald Walsch, Dr. Christiane Northrup, John Gray, Jack Canfield, and more. Abraham's work has also had a major impact on my life, and has heavily influenced the content and the lexicon of this book. I have integrated their teachings with my own guidance, observations, experiences, and clinical training as a psychotherapist. It is with great gratitude to Abraham-Hicks that I offer this book. This is my unique expression of timeless wisdom, to support you on your journey of bliss.

Our deepest and strongest desires are inspired by the part of us that resides in spirit and flows through us. This is known as our soul, or source energy. We came into this physical existence with deliberate intentions, which means that each of us has a destiny to fulfill while here. As we look for joy in our everyday experiences, we align with our destiny, the intent of our soul.

When we allow this pure vibration to flow through us, we can transcend the perceived limitations of the physical world. We can co-create—with source energy—unexpected, seemingly miraculous, and synchronistic events. We have access to the entire Universe because we are interconnected with everyone and everything. This is what Dr. Carl Jung referenced in his work regarding the collective unconscious and in his well-known paper and book *Synchronicity: An Acausal Connecting Principle*. He defined synchronicity as "a meaningful coincidence of two or more events, where something other than the probability of chance is involved."[1] All synchronicities in our lives stem from our interconnectedness with one another. By accessing the collective consciousness of the Universe, we tap into a stream of resources to fulfill our desires. The collective consciousness is like an ocean of thoughts, beliefs, and emotions of every living thing in the Universe that can guide and inspire us.

On the other hand, when our mind tells us that our desires are not realistic, or at best difficult to attain, we set up barriers that prohibit us from manifesting things that are important to us. For example, if we are yearning for a romantic partner and we focus our attention on feeling lonely, we create a vibration that attracts more reasons to feel lonely. Whatever we give attention to—consciously or unconsciously—becomes a magnet for the circumstances in our lives.

Introduction

This magnetic attraction is what we commonly refer to as romantic chemistry. As you read further, you will understand how vibrations are created and communicated to others. You will develop clarity about why you feel a magnetic attraction to some individuals and not to others. You will also learn how you can change your vibration to attract a different type of person, rather than let your past dictate your present circumstances.

As you begin this journey, simply set the intention that you will absorb the material in this book with an open mind. Allow yourself to understand and receive all that is in your highest good as you create the ideal relationship for you. By doing this you are commanding every cell in your being to assist you in aligning with your soul's intent. This alignment always brings forth success. You will become skilled at correlating your thoughts, feelings, beliefs, and experiences with your manifestations. With practice you will see an abundance of wonderful potential partners for you, regardless of your age, sex, or preferences.

Unlike many psychological or personal development books, *Tune into Love* does not tell you what you should or should not do, what is right or wrong, healthy or unhealthy. What you desire is your decision. You have the freedom to choose whatever relationship you want, and this book respects, nurtures, and fosters that right. By paying attention to your internal guidance system, and using the process of Vibrational Matching, you will learn how to develop clarity about what you want, and how to attract it.

The tools in this book will help you in all aspects of your life. You will be able to create enjoyable intimate relationships, good health, financial and career success along with other desires. As you work with these principles, you will become very powerful in manifesting the life you have always wanted. Your ability to manifest your dreams is limitless.

The Universe always fulfills our desires when the passion

is high, the intent is pure, and the "knowing" is strong. The concepts are simple, but the application is complex, explaining why so many people never make the shift from desiring a wonderful romantic relationship to actually creating it.

How to define, attract, and create the love of your dreams is the subject of this book. To inspire purposeful, passionate, and joyous living is the reason this book exists. It is offered to you from my heart and soul, and with great gratitude to the Universe. My wish is that you surround your dreams with the pure vibration of love and know that the perfect relationship for you is just around the corner. My entire being is with you on this great journey.

Part One

Create through
Consciousness

Tune into Love

What if fairies really do exist
throughout the Universe, in the mist,
to help us create our heavenly bliss?

What if one night while you were sleeping
your fairy Godmother came into your room peeking
while you were calm and peaceful and vividly dreaming?

What if your fairy Godmother handed you this book
and said, Here, take a very good look?

And what if your fairy Godmother said,
Let me help you to the other side of the fence.
Read this book to attract your princess, or prince?

And what if your fairy Godmother gave you one condition
that you must do to fulfill your intention
and in the next hour,
you will have your power?

Tune into Love

And what if you were willing to do
whatever she asked of you?

And what if that one condition was to look in the mirror and say,
I love you with all my heart and soul,
each and every day.
Oh, you wonderful being of light,
I will be true to you each and every night?

And what if your fairy Godmother waved her wand over you
and said,
As these words are spoken my dear,
your prince or princess will appear?

And what if you awoke
to see the back of a cloak
scurrying off into the night
amidst a bright light?

Only to find shimmers of fairy dust all over you
as you spoke these words, that rang so true.

And what if on your bedpost sat a white dove
holding a book called Tune into Love?

—Margaret McCraw, November 24, 2004

Chapter One
Attract through Vibration

*Expand in consciousness—be ready to accept
anything now, at any time.*

—Eileen Caddy

WHAT ARE VIBRATIONS?

For a brief moment, visualize yourself in a spaceship far out in the Universe, looking at all the planets and stars that surround you. You see patterns of energy moving in wave formations similar to patterns in the ocean. This movement of energy in wave formations is called vibrations. Each "space wave" consists of particles that vibrate at the same level. The rate of movement of these particles is known as frequency.

Particles within you project waves of energy. That energy expands outward from you in a cosmic dance, attracting and responding to frequencies of the same level in the Universe. All of life is a harmonious interaction with energy.

We all engage in this powerful process of transmitting and receiving vibrations, every moment of our lives. This energy exchange reflects back to us in the form of people and circumstances that we attract and allow into our life experiences—impacting finances, health, career, and our relationships.

You are perceived by the Universe as a vibration. Your thoughts, beliefs, and emotions make up your consciousness, which is interpreted by everything in the Universe as energy.

At one time it was believed that matter and energy were separate entities, but quantum physics has revealed that all matter, including human beings, pulsates with energy. Even the smallest particles of matter are not solid, but are actually compressed vibrating energy. In fact, everything vibrates at its own unique frequency, creating what we perceive as light, color, heat, solid matter, sound, and electromagnetic fields.

Sound waves cover a wide range of frequencies and are often undetected by our ears as well as being invisible to the human eye. Children can often hear higher frequencies than adults. Cats, dogs, and even dolphins have the ability to hear at a much greater range than humans. Even though humans cannot hear as wide a range of sounds as some animals, these frequencies are detected by our bodies, connecting us with energy that matches our own rates of vibration.

MAGNETIC ATTRACTION

Our bodies have an electrical system that responds to other vibrational frequencies. For example, when two frequencies are attuned to each other, they are said to be in resonance with each other. In resonance, the vibratory source produces waves that impart energy to objects and other living things. If these objects, individuals, or other life-forms have the same frequency, they will be set in motion too. Resonance is the fundamental principle of the Law of Attraction, or "like attracts like," which is universal and affects everything we attract.

In fact, when you strike the C string of a harp or violin, all the other octave strings of C begin to vibrate even though untouched by your hand. While other strings also absorb the energy of the plucked string, only those with the same frequency are set in motion.

THE PHYSICAL CHEMISTRY OF ROMANCE

During the early phase of romantic attraction, our bodies respond chemically by releasing neurotransmitters, which create a bright perspective on life, higher levels of energy, a fast pulse, and a sharper perception.[1] "The brain increases its production of endorphins and enkephalins, natural narcotics, enhancing a person's sense of security and comfort."[2] In the release of these powerful natural chemicals, romantic love is an intense physical experience that can truly be intoxicating.

THE PSYCHOLOGICAL CHEMISTRY OF ROMANCE

Each of us offers a distinct vibration for every desire we have. Our dominant vibration is what magnetizes our experiences, and is determined by the combined frequency of our thoughts, beliefs, and feelings regarding a particular desire. Romantic chemistry occurs because the dominant vibrational frequencies of two individuals are in resonance.

Most of us think that romantic chemistry is a mystery, but this is not true. When two individuals are in resonance, whatever they think, feel, and believe about themselves will be reflected back to them through each other. For instance, if you truly love yourself, you will feel a strong magnetic attraction to someone who can offer you genuine love. However, if you think you are unworthy of love, you will feel a strong magnetic attraction to someone who affirms this belief. If you think you are unattractive, you will resonate with someone who reinforces this belief. The stronger the resonance between two people, the stronger will be the chemistry or magnetic attraction.

Most of us are not conscious of the type of person with whom we resonate. For example, Renee met Lewis at a singles dance. She was very attracted to him the moment she saw him across the room, even though he did not match her usual preference for a tall, slender, and dark-haired man. Her heart immediately started palpitating as she began thinking of ways she could introduce herself. Once Renee struck up a conversation with Lewis, he was immediately captivated with her bubbly personality.

When they first started dating, Lewis was kind, considerate, and open to sharing intimate feelings. Renee was ecstatic about having attracted someone who seemed so different from men she had dated previously.

However, within six months of dating, things started to change rapidly. Lewis's thoughtfulness and openness became almost nonexistent. He wanted to stay home most evenings and watch television rather than spend time with Renee. He would promise that Saturday nights were "theirs" to do whatever they wanted, and then would decide at the last moment to rent a video of his choice, inviting Renee to watch it with him.

When Renee tried to talk with Lewis about her concerns, he would turn and walk away, leaving her more frustrated than ever. She started pressuring him persistently about spending more time together, which turned Lewis off and pushed him further away.

Renee has a long history of attracting men who are inconsistent in their ability to follow through with promises and in openly sharing their feelings with her. On the other hand, Renee is different from the type of man she usually attracts. She has a high degree of integrity; she is an excellent communicator and enjoys having intimate and in-depth conversations with a partner. However, her vibration is aligned with someone who lacks integrity and is emotionally unavailable,

because she focuses attention on her fear of attracting someone who does not have the attributes she desires.

For years since Renee's divorce, she has gone out to din-
ner with her friends each week and complained about her
frustrations with men. By focusing attention on the things
she does not want in a relationship, Renee has unconsciously
aligned her vibration to magnetically attract a man who mir-
rors her frustrations. She is, in fact, a perfect vibrational
match for what she fears, rather than what she desires.

Conversely, it was not surprising that Lewis attracted
Renee. He had ended a marriage a few years earlier, and was
angry and disheartened. It was not a coincidence that he and
Renee were magnetized to each other, for it was their dominant vibration of fear, anger, and discontent in their previous
relationships that brought them together.

DOMINANT VIBRATION

Persistent thoughts and beliefs about ourselves, in conjunction with strong emotion, become the dominate vibration that magnetizes romance.

The stronger and more positive our dominant vibration is
about a particular desire, the more quickly we will become a
vibrational match to it. There are three components to creating our dominant vibration.

   a. the frequency or intensity of the desire
   b. the frequency or feeling tone associated with the desire
   c. the frequency or strength of our belief associated with the
      desire

Clarity in conjunction with the level of enthusiasm for the
desire represents the intensity of the desire. For example,
how important is it to you that you attract a relationship?

The feeling tone, which can be positive or negative, is the
intensity of the passion associated with a particular desire.

For example, a positive feeling tone could be expressed as, "I am so excited that Paul and I are dating. I really like him a lot."

Belief is a factor in whether or not the feeling tone is positive or negative. If our belief is strong, then the feeling tone is more likely to be positive. If our belief is weak, then our feeling tone is more likely to be negative. For example, Sue told her best friend, "I'll never find someone who has the qualities I am looking for in a mate." In this example the feeling tone is negative and reflects a weak belief, which translates into a dominate vibration with a low frequency.

When we are *not* aware of our persistent thoughts and what we are giving attention to, we *unconsciously* create our dominant vibration, attracting our relationships. When we *are* aware of our thoughts, beliefs, and corresponding emotions with regard to ourselves and our romantic desires, we *consciously* create our dominant vibration, attracting our relationships.

Part 2 of this book teaches you how to *consciously* attract a romantic relationship by creating a vibration that magnetizes your desires. Becoming aware of your thoughts, beliefs, and corresponding emotions—as you correlate them with the relationships and experiences you are attracting—is a prerequisite for consciously creating what you desire.

While psychotherapy is not a prerequisite to becoming self-aware, it can be very helpful if the therapist understands vibrational alignment and helps you to: 1) identify your dominate vibration; 2) create resonance with your desires; and 3) reinforce your wholeness.

THOUGHTS AND EMOTIONS ARE LIVING THINGS

You might be asking yourself, how can my unspoken thoughts and hidden emotions affect the type of person I attract into my experience? Following are some examples of research on the power of thoughts and emotions.

Attract through Vibration

Dr. Masaru Emoto, author of *The Hidden Message in Water*, discovered from his worldwide research that vibrational energy in the form of thoughts, words, ideas, and music affects the molecular structure of water. Positive thoughts such as love and gratitude, as well as prayer, organized the water into a configuration resembling a snowflake, whereas negative thoughts created a chaotic pattern.

Dr. Emoto's photographs demonstrate that water is alive with energy, and highly responsive to our emotions and thoughts. This research has strong implications for humans, since our physical bodies are composed of at least 65 percent water. Humans and other living things, like water, absorb the vibrations projected onto them and respond accordingly by creating healthy or unhealthy patterns. The patterns we create are within our control.

Dr. David Hawkins, well-known psychiatrist and physician, used kinesiology, the study of muscles, to research high- and low-energy attractor fields to calibrate human consciousness. Hawkins demonstrated the ability of all human beings to influence the vibration of others through their thoughts. His research, spanning more than 20 years, is outlined in his book *Power vs. Force*.

Hawkins revealed that it is possible for individuals to make positive leaps in consciousness by choosing thoughts aligned with unconditional love. His research validates that the more we attune to a loving state of being, which is nonjudgmental and ever present, regardless of external factors, we align with the vibrational frequencies of the higher energy attractor fields.

In releasing (relinquishing) judgment, we can't help but magnetize loving energy around ourselves. Self-love—reflected in our level of confidence, sense of security, and self-esteem—is the powerful launching pad from which we attract love from others. If we feel loving toward ourselves, we attract others who feel the same way about us. If we feel unloving, fearful, or needy, we attract relationships that reinforce this vibration within us. What we vibrate *becomes* our reality. By cherishing and honoring ourselves, we have access to others who genuinely love us.

THOUGHTS ARE COMMUNICATED THROUGH PSYCHIC PHENOMENA

Since primeval times, people across cultures have reported profound psychic experiences that demonstrate a strong interconnectedness among all people.[3] Psychic phenomena, or what is sometimes called paranormal or psi (pronounced letter by letter: *p, s, i*), include telepathy, clairvoyance/remote viewing, precognition, extrasensory perception (ESP), psychokinesis, mental interactions with living organisms, and field consciousness. Related psychic phenomena include reincarnation; synchronicity; and life-after-death interactions such as clairaudience, out-of-body experiences (OBE), and near-death experiences (NDE). Table 1, located at the end of this chapter, defines specific psychic phenomena, giving examples and a brief update on current scientific research.

During the second half of the twentieth century, scientific research concluded that everything in the Universe is interconnected, demonstrated by more than a thousand experiments investigating psychic phenomena.[4] This interconnection is an important factor in understanding how our thoughts and beliefs, coupled with emotion—hence our vibration—are the basis for attracting our experiences. It also explains, scientifically, how each individual's vibration influences the vibration of others without regard to space and time. Reviewing the examples of psychic phenomena in table 1 will help you understand how this interconnectedness of all things and all people is interwoven within our daily lives. You will also come to realize that you have probably experienced and benefited from psychic phenomena many times in your life. In a 1987 survey, 67 percent of adults in the U.S. reported they had experienced psychic phenomena.[5]

In his book *The Conscious Universe*, Dean Radin tells us about Andrew Greeley, a sociologist at the University of Arizona who was curious about the psychological well-being of people reporting psychic experiences. Greeley decided to test these individuals using the Affect Balance Scale of psychological well-being, a standard psychological test used to measure healthy personality. Individuals tested received very high scores, indicating emotional/psychological health. According to the psychologist who developed the scale, there had been no other factor that had ever been found to correlate so significantly with well-being.[6]

Studies of psychic phenomena demonstrate that human potential has been severely underestimated, that science has just begun to understand the true nature of the Universe, and that outcomes that transcend reality, often referred to as "miracles," can easily be created by human consciousness.[7] Science has shown, without a doubt, that our mind is unlimited and that we are able to tune into a Universal consciousness that transcends our ordinary understanding of space and time. They are demonstrating, through research of psychic phenomena, the abundance of the Universe, and that we create our own reality through our vibration.

This is very exciting information and has an impact on all aspects of our life, specifically with regard to creating our dreams. No longer are we limited to thinking and believing that attracting love is by chance. No longer do we need to "buy into" the belief that there is a scarcity of eligible and desirable men and women. No longer do we need to wake up six months after we are married to discover that we attracted exactly what we did not want. We have control over our mind and our emotions, thus creating a vibration that gives us ultimate control over whom we magnetize romantically and otherwise.

Tune into Love

As you read this book and learn to raise your vibration, you are sending a clear signal to the Universe that you are open to assistance in fulfilling your desires. Be willing to say yes to all the help that arrives, and in doing so you will access the powerful universal consciousness. Assistance will arrive in ways you have not thought possible, including meaningful coincidences, sharpened intuition, telepathy, and perhaps other psychic phenomena. It is helpful to understand that experiences with psi are simply the Universe's way of acknowledging your intentions and offering help. Examples of others who opened up to messages from the Universe are provided below to prepare you for your own interactions with the higher, faster frequencies of the entire Universe, enabling you to attract your desires.

In 1930 Upton Sinclair, Pulitzer Prize-winning author, social activist, and a "no-nonsense realist," wrote the influential book *Mental Radio.* The book summarizes experiments that Sinclair and his wife performed, having to do with telepathy, clairvoyance, and precognition. Mrs. Sinclair had trained herself to become highly skilled at tuning into messages from the Universe, and this book describes their experiments. Albert Einstein reviewed and endorsed their research, as noted in the preface of *Mental Radio.*

Jose Silva, in his book *The Silva Mind Control Method,* tells a personal story about finances being tight just before he launched the Silva Method in the early 1960s. He explains that one night he dreamed of a bright light that had two sets of numbers below it. Silva told a friend about his dream and the friend suggested he buy a lottery ticket. Silva took his friend's suggestion and won $10,000 in cash, which he used to launch the internationally known Silva Mind Control method.

Silva also tells a story about a young widow with four children who did not have enough money for bus fare to take her children to the beach. The mother relaxed as she imagined them at the beach, and in a few minutes one of the children ran into the house and showed her a five-dollar bill that "just blew across the grass." This is another wonderful example of how assistance from the Universe shows up when we open ourselves to receiving. No desire is too small or too large.

While the focus of this book is to guide you in raising your vibration rather than developing your psychic skills, you will awaken your natural human intuitive psychic power, particularly your ability to create synchronistic events. As you heighten your awareness of how the integration of your thoughts, emotions, and beliefs creates your experiences, and in your willingness to shift to a higher vibration, meaningful coincidences will become routine in your day-to-day existence. Feelings of victimization will be left behind as you learn to take control of your life. This means taking responsibility for your life without judgment, guilt, or blame. Routine, objective observation of your experiences, and reflection on how you attracted them, will guide you to consciously fulfill your desires rather than your fears. Your world will become limitless, and you will attract fulfilling relationships as you allow assistance from the Universe.

Table 2 summarizes aspects of consciousness. It is based on a combination of scientific research, Jung's theories, Abraham-Hicks teachings, and my own clinical and personal experience and observations in working with consciousness. This information will guide you in understanding how thoughts, feelings, and emotions create our consciousness so you can raise your own vibration and attract the perfect relationship for you. I highly recommend that you review the information in table 2 before moving on to part 2 of this book, where you will learn how to align your frequencies to become a vibrational match for your desires. After you have read part 2, come back to this table and review it again, to help you understand the power of your consciousness to create your desires.

TABLE 1		
TYPES OF PHENOMENA LISTED BY SCIENTIFIC AND COMMON NAMES	**DEFINITION**	**EXAMPLES**
Telepathy	Communication between two or more minds without involving the usual everyday senses.	"Knowing" that your friend, whom you haven't spoken to in 10 years, is the one calling you on the phone without looking at caller ID.
Clairvoyance, Remote Viewing, Intuitive Medical Diagnosis	Clairvoyance is a French term meaning "clear-seeing." Information received without regard to distance and beyond the ability of our day-to-day senses to access this data.	Seeing the details of the contents of a building that is unfamiliar to you. Seeing the details of a living organism and being able to accurately identify and diagnose the body system that is out of balance.
Precognition, Second Sight, Premonition	Access to information about future events, where the information could not have been known by ordinary means. Often comes in the form of dreams and may also be referred to as prophecies or forewarnings.	Having a dream that your best friend meets a new guy while vacationing in the Bahamas and returns engaged. You don't mention this to her but three months later it actually happens.

PSYCHIC PHENOMENA AND CONSCIOUSNESS	
SCIENTIFIC EVIDENCE	**SCIENTIFIC RESEARCH**
YES	The Ganzfeld studies conducted from 1974 to 1997 are considered to be strong evidence for the existence of telepathy. The combined analysis produced a result with odds against chance of ten billion to one.[8]
YES	Stanford Research Institute (SRI) secretly studied psychic phenomena for the U.S. government during a 23-year period (1972–1995). Jessica Utts, a statistics professor at the University of California, and Dr. Ray Hyman, a known skeptic of psychic phenomena, carried out a government-sponsored review of the remote-viewing data. Both agreed that statistical results were "far beyond what is expected by chance," and that the studies were well designed using acceptable statistical and methodological procedures.[9] Edgar Cayce gave more than 14,000 clairvoyant readings until his death in 1945: 9,400 dealt with health issues. There is a library of documentation housed at the Association for Research and Enlightenment (ARE) in Virginia Beach, Virginia, that describes numerous cases in which Cayce described the exact condition and offered an herbal cure that was reported to be completely effective.[10]
YES	Combined results of 309 studies reported in 113 articles published from 1935 to 1987 with contributions from 62 different investigators demonstrated significant results with odds against chance of 10^{25} to one or ten million billion billion to one. The outcomes of these studies eliminated chance as a viable explanation.[11]

TABLE 1 (*CONTINUED*)		
TYPES OF PHENOMENA LISTED BY SCIENTIFIC AND COMMON NAMES	**DEFINITION**	**EXAMPLES**
Extrasensory Perception (ESP)	An everyday term that encompasses telepathy, clairvoyance, and precognition.	See examples cited for telepathy, clairvoyance, and precognition.
Mind-Matter Interaction, Telekinesis/Psychokinesis (PK)	Interaction that flows from mind to matter. Moving objects without having physical contact with them. Mental intention affecting matter.	You can bend a spoon by focusing mental attention on it and without touching it.
Mental Interactions with Living Organisms, Distant Mental Healing, Prayer	Interaction that flows from the mind to living organisms.	Applying focused positive thoughts to someone without necessarily having access to specific information; prayer involves asking for assistance from a higher power for yourself or someone else.

PSYCHIC PHENOMENA AND CONSCIOUSNESS	
SCIENTIFIC EVIDENCE	**SCIENTIFIC RESEARCH**
YES	See research cited for telepathy, clairvoyance, and precognition.
YES	The journal *Foundations of Physics*, 12/89, published an article describing 597 experimental studies and 235 control studies by 68 different investigators involving the influence of consciousness on matter. The analysis produced a result with odds against chance of 1 in 10^{35}.[12] The web site for Alternative Science describes this result in layman's terms: ". . . it is like finding a lottery ticket in the street, finding that it is the winning ticket and you have won first prize of millions—and then continuing to find the winning lottery in the street every week for a thousand years."
YES	A review of the literature in 1993 for cases of spontaneous remission of disease found 3,500 references in more than 800 medical and scientific journals in 20 languages.[13] A study by Fred Sicher, Elisabeth Targ, and others was published in the December 1998 issue of the *Western Journal of Medicine* describing the positive therapeutic effects of distant healing on men with advanced AIDS. Elisabeth Targ concluded, "Decreased hospital visits, fewer new severe diseases, and greatly improved subjective health supports the hypothesis of positive therapeutic effects of distant healing."[14] Larry Dossey, author of *Healing Words*, summarizes the following studies on prayer: "British psychic Matthew Manning held his hands near flasks containing cancer cells and focused attention on them in an attempt to inhibit growth. He was able to produce changes of 200 percent to 1,200 percent in their growth characteristics. He could also inhibit their growth from a distant room shielded from electrical influences."[15]

Tune into Love

TABLE 1 (CONTINUED)		
TYPES OF PHENOMENA LISTED BY SCIENTIFIC AND COMMON NAMES	**DEFINITION**	**EXAMPLES**
– – – – – – –	– – – – – –	– – – – – –
Field Consciousness	Groups of people focusing their minds on the same thing with the intention of influencing the outcome in the direction of their thoughts.	A group of individuals giving focused attention to world peace.

	PSYCHIC PHENOMENA AND CONSCIOUSNESS
SCIENTIFIC EVIDENCE	**SCIENTIFIC RESEARCH**
– – – – –	An article in the *Journal of the American Society for Psychical Research*, 1990, reveals a study by Dr. William Braud involving ordinary people mentally protecting red blood cells from serious, stressful influences. Findings suggest that healing thoughts can function at a distance regardless of whether they are directed to oneself or to another.[16] Cardiologist Randolph Byrd studied the effects of prayer in healing patients admitted to the coronary care unit at San Francisco General Hospital. His studies showed that patients prayed for differed from those not prayed for in several ways: 1) they were five times less likely to require antibiotics, 2) they were three times less likely to develop pulmonary edema, a condition in which the lungs fill with fluid, 3) unlike the control group none of the prayed-for group required insertion of a ventilator, an artificial airway inserted in the throat.[17] Daniel Benor, M.D., surveyed healing studies published in the English language prior to 1990. He found 131 studies, most of them in nonhumans. In 56 studies there was less than one chance in 100 that the positive results were due to chance. In another 21 studies, the potential for chance was between two and five in 100.[18]
YES	Studies conducted during the last decade evaluating the effects of field consciousness at the Consciousness Research Laboratory at the University of Nevada, Las Vegas, concluded that a deep interconnectedness between all things exists; some forms of synchronistic events can be planned using focused attention; the object of the focused attention does not seem to be important, only that it must hold the attention of the group; the effect of focused attention did not weaken with distance; global violence and aggression may stem from "chaotic, malevolent thoughts of large numbers of people around the world."[19]

TABLE 1 (CONTINUED)		
TYPES OF PHENOMENA LISTED BY SCIENTIFIC AND COMMON NAMES	DEFINITION	EXAMPLES
Out-of-Body Experiences (OBEs), Astral Projection, Astral Travel	Consciousness outside the physical body; the separation of one's energetic/astral body from the physical body; mental awareness and all senses are intact.	Being in a meditative state of mind (alpha mode) and feeling that you are in a room with your friend who lives 3,000 miles away. You can accurately describe the room and surroundings in detail even though you have never been there.
Near-Death Experiences	Consciousness outside the physical body (OBE) at the time of bodily death or immediately following.	A patient in a deep coma and in the process of being revived by CPR can later, upon survival, report detailed events that occurred, including describing equipment, conversations, and attitudes of doctors and nurses.
Reincarnation	Dying and being reborn into a new body with a new life and personality.	A five-year-old reports to his father that he remembers dying in a plane crash when he was 25 and the mother of two children. He gives his full name, his address in that lifetime, and the date of the crash, all verifiable information.

PSYCHIC PHENOMENA AND CONSCIOUSNESS

SCIENTIFIC EVIDENCE	SCIENTIFIC RESEARCH
Limited data available	Millions of people have reported OBEs, but relatively few have been clinically analyzed. In 1978 Dean Shiels studied approximately 70 non-Western cultures around the world. Of the 54 cultures that responded to the research, 46 percent claimed that most or all people could travel outside the physical body under certain conditions, 43 percent claimed that a few people could have OBEs, and only three cultures claimed that OBEs do not happen.[20]
Limited data available	December, 2004—The British medical journal *Lancet* published a Dutch study in which 344 cardiac patients were resuscitated from clinical death. About 12 percent reported seeing light at the end of a tunnel or speaking to dead relatives.[21]
YES	EEG studies show that children under five consistently exist in alpha mode, which is an altered state of consciousness in adults. They often report specific information about past lives that is verifiable. Adults routinely function in the beta mode of consciousness unless in a meditative state.[22]

TABLE 1 (*CONTINUED*)		
TYPES OF PHENOMENA LISTED BY SCIENTIFIC AND COMMON NAMES	**DEFINITION**	**EXAMPLES**
Life after Death Interactions, Clairaudience	Individual consciousness continues to exist after death of the body. Messages in thought forms from an entity existing in another realm beyond the range of the ordinary power of hearing. One "hears" what they are saying in their mind without auditory sounds.	Your deceased mother impresses thoughts on your mind to apply for a job in the marketing department at the local hospital. You inquire and discover that the perfect job for you has just become available. You find out the next day that your current position is being eliminated. Messages can be communicated directly or indirectly through a medium.
Synchronicity, Coincidences	A meaningful coincidence of two or more events, where something other than chance is involved. Consists of two factors: "a) an unconscious image comes into consciousness either directly or indirectly in the form of a dream, idea, or premonition; b) an objective situation coincides with this content."[25]	You dream about skiing in Switzerland and the next day your boyfriend unexpectedly presents you with a ticket to accompany him on a ski trip to Zurich, Switzerland.

PSYCHIC PHENOMENA AND CONSCIOUSNESS	
SCIENTIFIC EVIDENCE	**SCIENTIFIC RESEARCH**
YES	In highly controlled studies to eliminate interference or fraud, the University of Arizona evaluated information received by mediums from deceased individuals. The mediums achieved an overall accuracy rate of 83 percent. A control group of non-mediums was correct, on average, 36 percent of the time. Professor Gary Schwartz, research leader, summarized by saying, "The most parsimonious explanation is that the mediums are in direct communication with the deceased."[23] Nineteenth-century scholar F. W. H. Myers investigated mediumistic evidence for survival of individual consciousness after death. Documented evidence exists of accurate information being relayed to the mediums, sometimes in foreign languages that were unknown to the medium. These cases are discussed in his book *Human Personality and Its Survival of Bodily Death.*[24]
YES	Carl Jung presents evidence through his research and case studies in his book *Synchronicity: An Acausal Connecting Principle*, 1961.[26] Field consciousness studies reveal that meaningful relationships between mind and matter occur and that some forms of synchronistic events can be deliberately created.[27]

Tune into Love

TABLE 2

ASPECTS OF CONSCIOUSNESS

1. The power of an individual's consciousness is defined by one's ability to influence the order of things in the direction of his or her desires—or, simply put, to attract one's desires. This includes animate as well as inanimate objects.

2. The ability to influence the order of things in the direction of one's desires is derived from focused attention combined with clear intent. Therefore, the power of consciousness is derived from focused attention united with intention. Focused attention is defined as thoughts lined up in the same direction, creating a clear vision. Intention is defined as strong, clear desire, coupled with strong belief that you can attract your desire.

3. The amount of emotion that accompanies the intention is reflective of the strength of the desire. The strength of the desire impacts the power of an individual's consciousness.

4. The tone of the emotion that accompanies the intention reflects whether your belief is in alignment with your desire. If the emotion feels good to you, it indicates that your thoughts and beliefs about your desire are in alignment. If the emotion feels bad to you, it indicates that your thoughts and beliefs about your desire are not in alignment. Example: *Emotion that feels good—feeling enthusiasm as you look forward to attracting that special person into your life. Emotion that feels bad—feeling anxiety as you ponder the thought that "all the good women are taken."*

5. The power of an individual's consciousness directly affects the amount of time it takes to attract one's desires. The more powerful the consciousness, the more quickly the desire is attracted. As individuals increase their frequency levels, they have access to the larger database of the collective consciousness of the Universe.

Attract through Vibration

By accessing the collective consciousness of the Universe we tap into a stream of resources to fulfill our desires.

6. The power of an individual's consciousness is minimized by inconsistent thoughts. *For example: "I want to be in a committed relationship but I really like living alone."*

7. Consciousness extends beyond the individual and into the whole Universe.

8. Individual's consciousness is interconnected with the consciousness of everything else in the Universe. Individual consciousness is assimilated by the collective Universal consciousness.

9. Consciousness and the Universe are in constant motion, always expanding and evolving.

10. Consciousness exists within the magnetic fields of the Universe. Thoughts and feelings generate motion, which is called vibration. The rate of vibration, which is known as frequency, is how we communicate our thoughts and feelings throughout the Universe. *For example: a thought or vibration originating in New York can pass through a room in South Dakota without anyone seeing it and continue on to California. This thought is not seen with the eyes but it may be felt, depending on the frequency that is generated.*

11. Awareness of consciousness exists through vibration. Anything we attract into our experience is the result of the frequency of our vibration, which is our consciousness.

12. The higher the frequency, the less obstruction is attracted. *For example: a rock that is thrown and hits a building is stopped by the brick wall. On the other hand, a radio wave is a higher frequency than the rock so it will pass through the building without being obstructed. The frequency of thoughts is governed by the same Law of Attraction. For instance, the desire to be in a relationship when surrounded with thoughts of a lower vibration, such as fear, will prohibit you from meeting someone to whom you are attracted.*

13. The power of an individual's consciousness is minimized by resistance, which prevents access to desires.

Resistance is defined as fear. Fear comes in many forms, such as the things we worry about, defend against, prepare against, fight against, and struggle with.

14. Consciousness has power regardless of whether focused attention occurs in consecutive blocks of time or is interspersed with other thoughts throughout an extended period of time.

15. A group of individuals creates group consciousness. The group does not have to be located in the same physical space to be considered a group. The power of the group's consciousness is in proportion to the strength of focused attention united with intention.

16. All aspects of individual consciousness apply to group consciousness.

17. Consciousness is immortal. Death is applicable only to the physical body.

18. Consciousness is reality. As we have clarity about our desires and focus our attention on our intentions rather than our fears, we vibrate at a higher frequency. A higher frequency gives us easier access to the collective consciousness of the Universe, which is the source of all our desires. As we maintain a high frequency, we tune into and allow assistance from the Universe.

19. Consciousness exists on multiple levels throughout the Universe. These levels are determined by vibrational frequency. Freedom and joy are attained in proportion to the rate of our vibrational frequency of consciousness. The higher the frequency, the greater the levels of freedom and joy we experience.

Chapter Two
Vibrational Matching

Thoughts cause vibrations that set in motion the manifestation of reality.

—Author Unknown

What is Vibrational Matching? To understand Vibrational Matching you must first understand the term "vibrational match." Each of us attracts into our experience people, places, and things that vibrate at the same frequency as our thoughts, beliefs, and feelings. Whatever we focus our attention on is reflected in the circumstances of our life. This is the Law of Attraction. Whatever we attract, whether it is wanted or unwanted, is *always* a vibrational match for the energetic signals we send out into the collective consciousness of the Universe.

Vibrational Matching is the deliberate intention to attract our desires—in this case, a romantic relationship—by aligning and focusing our thoughts, emotions, and beliefs with what we want. In other words, it is drawing in a desired outcome by sending out harmonious energy that will bring it in. In so doing, we are able to easily attract our desires, because

Tune into Love

the Universe will respond to our alignment of energy through the powerful Law of Attraction. Refer to exhibit A to more fully understand Vibrational Matching.

EXHIBIT A   VIBRATIONAL MATCHING

Your thoughts, beliefs, and feelings can go in one of two directions, either having your desire or not having your desire. Your dominant vibration for any desire is a culmination of frequencies of your thoughts, beliefs, and feelings associated with the desire.

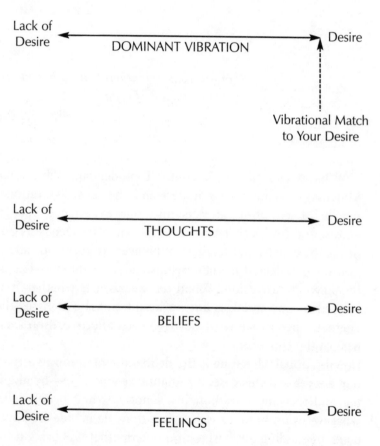

Vibrational Matching

This may sound simple, but it takes practice to fine-tune this process. As we all know, we can "wish" all we want, but we will not necessarily get what we desire by wishing alone. In fact, most of our thoughts go out in random form without any real force or focus behind them. Thoughts that bring in a desirable vibrational match are always accompanied by strong, positive emotions. This is one of the factors for success that will speed the desire to its fruition.

When our desirous thoughts, such as, "I would love to meet someone special," are coupled with fears, the chances are slim of receiving what we want. Pessimistic inner chatter such as, "There are no good men left," or statistics focusing on receding chances for marriage after age 35 can get in the way of sending out a desire with the optimistic "wings" necessary to manifest it.

For instance, if a woman believes deep down that she will never find the right guy, she will not be a vibrational match for creating a desirable partnership. When she changes her belief about herself and sees herself as deserving, she will be much more likely to attract someone who believes that too.

By understanding the Universal Law of Attraction and the Vibrational Matching techniques that allow us to purposefully create what we want, whether it is a healthy body, more money, a new home, or the perfect mate, we can take charge of our lives and our happiness. Once you master this technique, you will become the creator of your life experiences.

As you learn to focus your thoughts on your desires, rather than on what you lack, you will no longer experience scarcity. By practicing the techniques of Vibrational Matching, you will have access to the abundance of the Universe. As you become the architect of your future, you will find that choices will appear along the way. Everything you wish for is possible to receive. Correlating your thoughts, feelings, and beliefs with what you attract will inspire you to give more attention to what you desire.

As you begin to make the connection between what you

think, how you feel, and what you attract, you will come to an understanding of how Vibrational Matching works. You will also realize that you are in control of what you bring in to your experience, and that you can make choices that are aligned with what you desire rather than what you fear.

Our thoughts are vibrant energies that we project out into the Universe. When they are supercharged with emotion, they gain even more power. For example, when someone is overjoyed because they received a raise at work, or got a date with Mr. Wonderful, the world becomes a magical place—at least, for a while. More positive experiences seem to follow in rapid succession. Ever wonder why good things sometimes come in a series? It is as if that person has truly been blessed.

The power of human thought has long been recognized by both scientists and psychologists. Scientist Marcel Vogel discovered that even plants could pick up on human thoughts. When the plants felt threatened, they released certain vibrations picked up on a special meter. Dr. Deepak Chopra points out that our minds influence every cell in our bodies. When we are depressed, our immune systems plummet. By the same token, feeling love can restore them to a healthy level. Dr. Bernie Siegel discovered that replacing fear with love could heal our bodies as well as increase our lifespans. He gives numerous examples in his books of how we can rid ourselves of illness and create our health, regardless of the medical prognosis.

We all know how good it is to be on a "natural high." Take Jill, for instance. Today, on a happiness scale of one to ten, Jill is an eight. Everything seems to be going her way. As she relishes her successes, her elevated vibration affects every thought that flows from her, drawing in other level-eight experiences. People seem nicer, things go more smoothly, and Jill's problems seem to disappear, at least for now.

Should Jill's thoughts turn negative, they will attract similar energies and experiences from others. Even her body will respond to her thoughts: her hormone levels may drop, her sleep may be interrupted, her blood may be more prone to clotting, and, should she shed a tear, it will have a different chemical component from tears of joy.

Jane is an example of a pessimistic thinker. She has convinced herself that there are very few attractive single men in her age group. She reinforces this belief every Friday night when she and her girlfriends get together at a local lounge to let off steam. Jane does not realize that venting is counterproductive to attracting her desires.

Today, she was particularly annoyed when Gary, one of her office mates, chose not to join her in the cafeteria after she had waved him over. As Jane dwells on her hurt feelings, she projects them with great emotion. Right now, she is not a vibrational match for attracting a positive relationship.

Part 2 of this book will reveal how to set forth your intention to receive what you wish and will guide you through a unique, highly successful technique to help you manifest your wishes for a loving partner. This method works because it blends your "passionate intention" with a clear, step-by-step approach to raise your personal vibration. In this way, you will draw in the ideal relationship for you.

Now that you understand you can have it all, you can "go for the gold"—a satisfying, happy relationship that fulfills all your desires. The best way to achieve this is to be confident and clear when you are projecting your thoughts. Psychologists have known for years that a low self-image can actually prevent us from being able to attract a desirable relationship. However, they have not really understood the principles of Vibrational Matching—that everyone has a personal vibratory level that reflects their thoughts, beliefs, and emotions. When we learn to view life circumstances optimistically, as well as to align our beliefs with our desires, our personal vibration begins to strengthen, enabling us to attract more positive experiences.

For example, Susan, a 32-year-old nurse, is unclear about what she wants. Her relationship with Sean, of eight months, has just ended. Susan believes that Sean left her because she was ten pounds overweight and therefore, she believes, less attractive than she was when they met. Sean disagreed, simply claiming he needed "space" for a while. While Susan misses Sean, she is not even sure she would want him if he returned.

As Susan gains confidence in herself, and sets clear intentions of what she desires, she will project a higher and more positive vibration. This will enable her to attract a more satisfying and fulfilling relationship.

DRAW A MENTAL PICTURE

Rebecca is a creative, independent 36-year-old painter whose heart was broken after her marriage failed. Realizing she was at a personal crossroads, she learned about Vibrational Matching, and immediately took steps to attune herself to attract exactly what she wanted in a partner.

Rebecca created a very detailed Wish List to help her draw a mental picture of the man she wanted to attract into her life. She particularly wanted someone who could be a loving father for her three-year-old son, Tyler, as well as a gentle, sensitive partner for herself. Rebecca then activated the Four Frequencies, which you will learn about in part 2 of this book, to tune in to a partner who would match her desires. Within a month, she met Rod at an art show.

Rod, a warm, sensitive gallery director, had never married but longed to have a family. He immediately responded to Rebecca's dynamic personality. Rebecca was drawn to Rod, too, but needed to be sure that Rod and Tyler would hit it off. A year later, Rod and Rebecca moved in together, after it was clear that Rod was a vibrational match for her desires for her son as well as for herself.

This match worked because Rebecca was very clear about the kind of partner she wanted to attract. In turn, she got exactly the kind of relationship she intended.

REPETITIVE PATTERNS

However, if energies are sent out at random, without being open to one's highest good, old patterns can repeat themselves. For instance, Stan and Suzy are a good example of how old patterns repeat themselves. A successful real estate salesman, Stan just walked away from his third divorce. He is charming, financially secure, and bright. However, Stan has a belief system that creates unhappiness in his relationships. He believes that relationships are not built to last. While Stan falls in love quickly, after six months the bloom is off the rose and he begins to stray.

Thrice married, he is now single again and looking for a new partner. Enter Suzy, whose track record is not aligned with her desire to have a long-term, loyal partnership with a loving man. Her last two relationships were with men who were unfaithful. Now, she desperately wants to find a man who will be committed to her and monogamous. Her feelings of desperation reflect a lack of confidence in herself and keep her at a low vibration. She is not a match for what she says she wants. Suzy continues to sabotage her chances by focusing on her fears. "I will never trust a man again," she tells her friends. "They are all cheaters at heart."

Still, Suzy goes out with a variety of men to see if she might, despite her fears, find Mr. Right. When she meets Stan at a party, they are immediately drawn to each other. After being wined and dined nonstop for two weeks, Suzy finds herself hoping that Stan just might be the one to break the pattern. Maybe he will not cheat on her. Maybe he will be her desirable match.

But as time passes, Stan's belief system—that relationships are not built to last—proves to be solidly in place, and predictably, the relationship comes to an unhappy ending. Now, Suzy, again hurt and angry, is reinforced in her belief that men cannot be trusted.

Yet the energies Suzy was sending out did indeed bring her

a perfect vibrational match. By focusing attention on her fears, she energetically aligned with what she did *not* want, causing this vibration to be projected stronger than her desire for a man of integrity. Stan, a perfect vibration for Suzy's fears because of his own beliefs, unconsciously responded to the energy she was sending out to the Universe: "They're all cheaters at heart."

This type of scenario is being played out every day, as romantic intentions find themselves thwarted time and again. Even when a relationship starts out well and seems to be overriding past patterns, the honeymoon period eventually ends and the pattern that brought in the relationship asserts itself. However, once people learn how to use the principles of Vibrational Matching, these pitfalls fail to arise.

THE MOON IS IN THE WRONG POSITION . . .

Although most people say they want to find "the right person" to fulfill their desires for a partner, sometimes resistance can occur, even without the person's conscious knowledge. Let's look in on Jade's situation as she talks with her therapist about her desire for a relationship. Jade's strong beliefs in the power of such forces as astrology are reflected in her conversation with her therapist below:

"It's not a good time for me to find a partner," she told her therapist ruefully. "In fact, I'm under a three-year cycle of isolation. My astrologer told me I will not attract a relationship until it's over. However," she admitted, "I'm so lonely. I do not know what to believe."

The fact that Jade had been inspired to seek counseling was evidence that she wanted to reach out, despite the astrological issues. When she realized that she had the power to control what she attracted into her life, regardless of her astrological chart, she took a deep breath and decided to try Vibrational Matching.

Resistance can show up in many forms. It is important to be aware of the barriers we create that delay and prevent us from attracting our desires. All perceived barriers can be dissolved by Vibrational Matching if the individual genuinely wants to overcome them.

You Are Your Own Best Matchmaker

"Matchmaker, matchmaker, make me a match," goes the song. Why put yourself in another person's hands when you are the only one who can really get the job done? When Vibrational Matching for the desired outcome is undertaken under optimum conditions, here's how it works:

- An individual, or "the sender," has a clear desire for a partner. "Clear" means that the sender has given much thought to the desired qualities of a potential partner.

- Once "the sender" has carefully selected these qualities, he or she is ready to release the desire to attract the right person, setting the intention for the highest good for all concerned.

- The release is accompanied by a deep, confident "knowing" that the desired vibrational match will be attracted.

- A desire is set forth as a thought vibration, that the match be attuned to "the highest good" of both parties.

- The "sender's" vibratory message is energetically received and accepted by a partner vibrating at the same level.

- The "sender" and the "receiver" meet when the time and conditions are aligned with "their highest good," which is *always* when they are ready to receive the desire they have manifested.

Both sender and receiver are active vibratory participants in this process. The sender is consciously involved, while the receiver may be participating on a conscious or unconscious level. Both are co-creators of this experience because energetically, they always attract thought vibrations aligned with their own.

Since the Universe offers an abundance of choices, it can deliver more than one desirable vibrational match to the sender. Think of the Universe as the ultimate computer—one that has the ability to filter, sort, and bundle all the vibrational signals it receives and deliver it to the perfect vibratory match. Whatever you are focused upon will be attracted into your experience. If you focus upon a particular desire, you will attract it. However, if you focus upon what is missing in your life, you will attract more experiences reinforcing what is lacking. The Universal Law of Attraction always ensures that our experiences are in alignment with our thoughts and beliefs. So if we believe that all the "good men" are taken, we will only attract men whom we perceive to be undesirable. On the other hand, if we understand that there is more than one right partner for each of us, we will tap into the abundance of the Universe. If we believe there are men who are both desirable and available, we will attract infinite opportunities to date Mr. Right. There is no escaping the Law of Attraction.

In part 2, this wonderful process of Vibrational Matching will be explored in more detail. What is important for you to know is that Vibrational Matching works because you have the ability to purposefully attract a partner whose desires are harmonious with your own desires. The knowledge of how to make this happen is the gift this book brings to you.

Chapter Three

Awaken to a Higher Guidance

The intellect has little to do on the road to discovery. There comes a leap in consciousness, call it intuition or what you will, and the solution comes to you, and you don't know how or why.

—Albert Einstein

INTUITION

Intuition is derived from the Latin word *intueri*, which means to "look within" or to "regard inwards." Intuitive knowledge is transmitted from a higher, faster, vibrational frequency than the physical plane. It is information that comes to us from the collective consciousness of the Universe, which all of us have the ability to access. Our soul, or source energy, is part of the collective consciousness that flows through us. When we look within we are accessing the wisdom of our soul as well as the wisdom of the greater whole. Once we raise our level of vibration, we can more easily tune into the guidance that surrounds us.

Intuition is a type of psychic phenomenon. It expresses itself through our senses and can be received in various ways including telepathy, clairvoyance, clairaudience, or precognition. It can even be the result of field consciousness (refer to table 1 at the end of chapter 1). If you have experienced intuition, and no doubt you have, then you have also experienced psychic phenomena. As Albert Einstein indicated in the above quote, these flashes of insight do not stem from logic, intellect, or reasoning of the conscious mind. Instead, they are a powerful knowing that guides us to our highest good.

Today, more than ever, we recognize the value of easily accessing answers to challenging questions, giving us a sense of control over our lives. Most of us have been taught to use our rational mind to guide us in decision-making and to derive answers in a logical way. Few individuals have been taught to use their intuitive mind, although many do indeed use it, whether they know it or not.

We refer to intuition by many different names. Some of these common references are listed below:

- a gut feeling
- a strong feeling
- a knowing
- a hunch
- sixth sense
- inspiration
- flash of insight
- an inner voice
- something we sense
- an idea that comes out of the blue
- message from an unknown source
- message from the soul
- message from a guardian angel
- message from God/Goddess
- message from a family member or friend in spirit

Everyone has access to this guidance, but many individuals minimize its power to help us because of its intangible and mysterious nature. While using our intuition is a very natural process, our rational mind, and the world at large, often convinces us that credible decisions can be made using only data and facts. Whenever possible, we can benefit from integrating our rational mind and our intuitive guidance; however, I have found that intuition frequently contradicts the logic of the rational mind, requiring that you choose one or the other. Going the intuitive route often requires a leap of faith and therefore a risk; however, the rewards can be great. As we acknowledge our wholeness as individuals, we naturally become more acutely aware of our intuition. In trusting the wisdom of the guidance it brings us, happiness will be ours.

How Can Intuition Help You?

Intuition can help you attract desires of all kinds, including the love relationship of your dreams. It can help you make daily decisions, both big and small, as well as inspire you to be creative. It can guide you to the fulfillment of your destiny. It can help you solve simple and complex problems. It can even guide you when you are not asking direct questions, if you have an open mind.

When we are guided by intuition we are allowing the Universe to help us. This means that instead of going 'round and 'round in circles trying to accomplish something, we can instead attract whatever is needed to help us.

In Vibrational Matching, believing in yourself and following your intuitive guidance to inspire you into action are two key ingredients for success. In conjunction with other techniques for raising your frequency level outlined in part 2 of this book, this will ensure that you will attract the love of your dreams. The following examples demonstrate how I used intuition to attract love relationships.

Tune into Love

During the summer of 1995 I was very busy with my work. I was not dating anyone at the time and had little time to go to social gatherings because of pressing work issues. I had planned to attend an out-of-town business seminar, but at the last moment I decided to cancel in an effort to meet a project deadline. My rational mind was clear about my decision to cancel, as I thought: Stay home and finish this report. However, as I picked up the telephone to cancel my flight, I "heard" an inner voice say, "Do not cancel, there is someone attending this training that you will want to meet." The message was strong, clear, and came out of the blue. I followed my guidance and needless to say, the first night on the trip I met Ron, a wonderful man whom I began dating, sharing wonderful moments of romance, friendship, and laughter.

On another occasion I created a Wish List of all the attributes of a man I wanted to attract for an intimate relationship. I created sacred energy around my desires by lighting a candle, saying a prayer, and putting good thoughts around my desires. A week later, while I was meditating, I received an intuitive message: You will find the one of your desires by going to a place where people "think the way you think." I asked myself the question: Where do people have beliefs that are similar to my own? The answer came immediately: I followed my guidance and that week, as I walked into the community meeting house to hear a talk, Tom was there to greet me. Tom and I had been introduced ten years before during a business meeting. He was happily married at the time, and expecting a child. Now, divorced for four years, he was ready to begin a new relationship, which we did at once.

DEVELOP YOUR INTUITION

Be Open-Minded

When we release judgments such as "right/wrong" or "black/white" thinking, we open ourselves to possibilities in all areas of our lives. Releasing limited thinking allows us to operate at a higher vibrational frequency, thereby tuning into the wisdom of the collective consciousness of the Universe.

Be Optimistic

The Law of Attraction will ensure that we magnetize whatever we focus our attention on, so if we are optimistic we open ourselves up to possibilities. When we are pessimistic we literally "shoot ourselves in the foot," and prohibit ourselves from attracting our desires. Being optimistic allows guidance to come forth in the form of intuition and synchronistic events, gently nudging us in the direction of our desires.

Be Honest with Yourself and Others

As you release judgments of yourself and others you will find that telling the truth becomes easier. When we tell "half truths" or "white lies" we are operating from a place of fear. Honesty clears a direct path to the higher truths of the Universe that come in the form of intuition.

Be Free of Drama

As we practice telling the truth, the drama in our lives cannot survive. Drama stems from the "stories" we tell ourselves that keep us from moving forward in the direction of our desires. Drama stems from fear, a belief in scarcity, and a lack of self-respect. As we practice accepting and appreciating ourselves, a life of integrity and fulfilled dreams will replace the theatrics in our day-to-day existence.

Tune into Love

Be Fully Present

Be aware of your surroundings and pay attention to what you are experiencing through all of your senses. Take time each day to slow down; still your mind and be comfortable with silence. Connect your thoughts with your feelings and notice which thoughts create a sense of well-being. Pay attention to your communications with others and make an effort to listen thoughtfully to the verbal and nonverbal cues in all your interactions.

Being fully present will help you feel more appreciative and to become aware of the synchronicities in your life. You will start to feel that your life has more meaning, and the big picture of your destiny will begin to reveal itself in those quiet moments of reflection.

Be Playful and Lighthearted

Be like a small child rejoicing over the simple pleasures of life. Create time in your busy schedule to laugh, seeing humor whenever possible. Smile a lot, and notice people smiling at you, as it is a wonderful gift to both give and receive. Take time to use your playful imagination, seeing greater possibilities wherever you can.

Be Free of Clutter

Let go of things in your house, your office, and in your heart that no longer represent who you are. As you clear out things that no longer serve you, an opening is created in your consciousness to allow your new desires to come to fruition. Holding on to things that have negative connotations or simply do not "fit" who you are will prohibit you from attracting your desires.

Pay Attention to Your Dreams

During sleep we are connecting with our soul and with the collective consciousness of the Universe. Our mind is sorting through our daily experiences and helping to prepare us for the next day. By becoming aware of our dreams, we open ourselves to guidance that can have very practical implications in solving challenging situations and creating desires. Remembering and interpreting our dreams is a process that becomes more meaningful as we engage in it with regularity. Follow the procedure below to enhance the guidance that comes through your dreams and that is available to you on a daily basis.

HOW TO RECEIVE GUIDANCE FROM YOUR DREAMS

1. Before you go to sleep, tell yourself that you will remember your dreams—whatever is in your highest good to remember. If you have a particular question about which you would like guidance, write that question down. Set the intention to receive and remember information that is in your highest good.

2. Keep a notebook and pen by your bed, and when you wake up, start writing. Even if you do not think you can remember your dreams, just write about anything. As you write, you may actually begin to remember your dreams.

3. Stay in bed and write instead of moving to a new location. Moving disrupts the process and can make it more difficult to remember your dreams.

4. After you have recorded the dream, ask the Universe for guidance on what the dream means and start writing whatever comes to you.

5. Pay attention to images and symbols and write your interpretation of them. If you have no idea what they mean, stretch your imagination and write whatever comes to mind.

As you do this process daily, you will strengthen your intuitive guidance, not just through your dreams, but in meaningful messages that come to you during the day. In your willingness to regularly access information from your dreams, you create a vibration that attracts and engages the assistance of the Universe.

MEDITATION—WHAT IS IT?

We meditate as a means of staying in alignment with the pure vibration of our soul. When we meditate we also open ourselves up to guidance from the collective consciousness of the Universe, and in so doing, strengthen our intuitive skills. By meditating we allow each day to unfold with calm awareness and new insights. In meditation we receive guidance from the Universe, whereas in prayer we talk to the Universe. Both are helpful in opening up to the fullness of life and remaining present as we go throughout each day.

Meditation can help us:

- Relax and stay calm
- Enhance our intuitive skills
- Receive guidance about steps to take to create our desires
- Align our mental, emotional, spiritual, and physical energies
- Stay healthy
- Minimize and release stress
- Connect with our emotions

WHY MEDITATE?

Consistent meditation helps us to perceive our world from a higher perspective. It increases our ability to give ourselves wholeheartedly to any task requiring attention, as well as to our relationships. This higher vision enables us to be more efficient, effective, joyful, and loving throughout the day. We bring a zest to life, and a passion for our purpose, as opposed to living our life by going through the motions. We allow ourselves to be inspired into action, and to be more efficient in managing our time. Our lives become synchronized in a beautiful and loving way, and we are centered and able to appreciate these meaningful coincidences. Meditating helps us attract a strong sense of well-being.

How to Meditate

Meditation is a skill that develops with regular practice. I find it helpful to allow at least 30 minutes in the morning and 30 minutes in the evening for this practice. Meditating in the morning strengthens us as we face challenges in a new day. Meditating at night helps us to gain insights about our day and close with a peaceful, restful sleep so that we can wake up refreshed in the morning.

Prepare to meditate by:

- Creating a comfortable environment that is quiet with no distractions
- Holding a comfortable posture
- Wearing comfortable clothes

The Process of Meditating

There are many schools of thought on meditating and many wonderful books dedicated to the subject. I would highly encourage you to explore these resources and find a method that works for you. However, the basic approach usually involves clearing our mind of busy thoughts, allowing us to receive insightful messages from the Universe. This can be done through a variety of methods, including a guided meditation in which someone takes us on a journey through self-exploration. Other methods may include sitting quietly in a comfortable position and focusing on a single thought, such as our breathing or the flame of a candle, or repeating a mantra such as AH or OM.

Tune into Love

We can create a walking meditation by taking slow, deliberate steps and focusing on a simple word, such as Joy, Abundance, or Peace. We can also meditate by lying down, sitting, or standing, and slowly and deliberately focusing on various parts of our body. We may extend our thought by sending love to our head, our neck, and our shoulders and moving downward toward our feet.

In a freestyle meditation—in which a single thought is the focus—we may keep our eyes opened or closed, depending on what is most comfortable for us. We may find that our head moves about gently in a circular motion and that images or messages are impressed on our mind. Many times I will get an answer to a question I've posed to the Universe, such as: Is it in my highest good to accept a particular speaking engagement? Guidance may come in the form of a picture, symbols, or thoughts. You can also ask yes or no questions, and the movement of your head will determine the answer coming from higher guidance. For example, in my meditations an up-and-down movement of my head signifies yes, and a side-to-side movement signifies no.

Sometimes when I meditate, a great deal of information will come in a single moment. It feels like a page of information has been downloaded and stamped on my brain—without words. There are also times when I meditate that I don't receive visual images or messages. It is simply a quiet period of time. It is important to realize that all outcomes from meditating are positive. We must remain open in order to receive whatever is in our highest good.

It is important to create a meditation routine that feels comfortable. Trying various techniques, as well as taking formal classes, listening to guided meditations on CDs, using a visual aide such as a mandala, or reading books, will support you in developing a plan that works best.

MANDALA

*I realized more and more clearly that the
mandala is the center; it is the expression of
all life; it is the path of individuation.*
—Carl Gustav Jung

Mandalas are pictorial representations of symbolic images, and are found among all people and all cultures. Mandalas are a sacred art form that symbolizes wholeness, and are in the shape of a square or a circle. According to Carl Jung, in his book *Mandala Symbolism*, "They are yantras in the Indian sense—instruments of meditation, concentration, and self-immersion—for the purpose of realizing inner experience. At the same time they serve to produce inner order. . . . They express the idea of a safe refuge, of inner reconciliation and wholeness." Jung studied these symbols for fourteen years before he began interpreting them. He encouraged his clients to create their own mandalas and then interpreted the symbols for them, helping them to tune into the guidance of the collective consciousness of the Universe.

In his book *Memories, Dreams, and Reflections*, Jung tells how he personally used the mandala for self-exploration. "I sketched every morning in a notebook a small circular drawing, a Mandala, which seemed to correspond to my inner situation at the time. With the help of these drawings I could observe my psychic transformations from day to day. . . . Only gradually did I discover what the mandala really is: 'Formation, Transformation, Eternal Mind's eternal recreation.'[1] And that is the self, the wholeness of the personality, which if all goes well is harmonious, but which cannot tolerate self-deceptions."

Figure A is a mandala that I commissioned specifically for this book as a gift to the reader. It is entitled "Divine Union," and is an inspired and original work of Marius Michael-George. I commissioned this artwork with the clear intention that the reader could meditate on this sacred image and tune into the vibration of love specific to your desires. Each individual will attune to the mandala differently, creating your relationship dreams. Individual messages aligned with your highest good will come to you during your meditation. The colors in the mandala are vibrant and beautifully displayed throughout the image. Go to my web site listed in the back of this book for information on ordering a colored mandala for personal use in meditation.

Jayne Howard, author of *Commune with the Angels*, specializes in interpreting ancient symbols specific to mandalas. I commissioned Jayne to work with me on interpreting the symbols in this mandala and to create an inspired guided meditation.

Below is information on the symbols and colors of the mandala in figure A.

Interpretation of shapes/numbers:

- Triangle—supreme power and blessings of abundance; it is a configuration of pure vibration taking shape and manifesting prosperity; also a symbol of protection.
- Triangle pointed up—this is the original icon for male and represents manhood; formally known as the blade.
- Triangle pointed down—this is the original icon for female and symbolizes femininity, womanhood, and fertility; formally know as the chalice.
- Triangle pointed up blended with one pointed down— perfect union of masculine and feminine energies; as above so below; yin-yang.
- Six-pointed star—star of love and true peace; symbol of the dynamic force and true light that overcome fear and unhappiness; represents a perfectly balanced life; man/woman made perfect; a blending of heaven and earth or spirit and matter; it is known as the Star of David.
- Four—the six-pointed star appears four times in ascending order, meaning "worlds within worlds" or "dimensions within dimensions"; four means a blessing of

FIGURE A

divine order flowing from heaven and earth; four planes of consciousness (physical, mental, emotional, and spiritual; or fire, air, water, and earth). A union with another individual on all four levels—physical, mental, emotional, and spiritual—can never be broken.

- Circle—the Infinite Mind of the All, or the all-encompassing energy of Universe; a metaphysical doorway to God Mind and Oneness.

- Seven Interlaced Circles—"the seed of life"; creation, procreation; cell division; propagation of life itself.

- Vesica piscis—this is the common area shared by two identical circles which implies mutual understanding; this symbol is made by intersecting two identical circles of the same size that share the same radius; the intersection of these two circles symbolizes common ground, shared vision, or mutual understanding between two equal individuals; the shape of the human eye is in the form of a vesica piscis, which implies "seeing eye to eye."

The vibration of colors:

- Purple—spiritual freedom, liberation, enlightenment, transformation taking place
- Aqua—letting go of ego and allowing the pure vibration of the Universe to be the center point of your being
- Green—healing, growth, evolution, expansion
- Deep pink—divine love or unconditional love, and adoration
- Yellow—wisdom, illumination, understanding
- White—goodness, purity, eternalness
- Rays of white light—pulsations from the points of light; light beams, love beams, shining forth upon all who gaze into the mandala

Below is an inspired meditation offered by Jayne Howard specifically for this mandala. I suggest listening to some soothing music and contemplating the words. Read them slowly, and allow yourself to go into a deep meditative state. Do this daily to help you tune into the love you desire.

Meditation

As you meditate upon the mandala, you become aware of the presence of Angels—Guardians of the Threshold of Eternal Freedom. Their presence is revealed to you by the pulsating points of white light that radiate transcendent energies, vibrations, and consciousness. These angelic energies amplify and intensify your own divine nature within. Their light draws you deeper into a sacred space of self-understanding. The mandala takes on the form of a cosmic mirror. You are seeing your own soul's reflection with light sight. You are seeing yourself through the eyes of the divine.

As your mind explores the glorious colors, dynamic geometric shapes and forms of the mandala, your soul stirs with the excitement of self-discovery. The shapes mirror to you the freedom you have to shape your own life. The apexes of the triangles speak to your soul of the highest ideals that are the core essence of your being. The integration of the shapes activates within you bridges of understanding that you are expressing yourself in more than one realm simultaneously. There are worlds within worlds inside of you. You are multidimensional, multi-universal. You have come into this world with a spiritual mission and purpose that you now clearly see. Your own uniqueness is mirrored back to you by the light of all.

As you continue to gaze into the mirror of all—the eye of the divine—you experience an initiation into the sacred mysteries of your life. What was once invisible is made visible. Invisible mental faculties, heightened sensitivities, and powers are now activated. The mandala draws you deeper and deeper into the cosmos of your being. In this place of oneness with the infinite, you experience a sense of your soul's mission. Waves of insight wash over you as you break through conditioned thinking and experience the hidden wisdom of your soul. The mandala takes you to a place of anointing. You are anointed with the awareness that your life is a blessing of unlimited potential—infinite freedom and possibilities.

The mandala overflows with the energies of eternal movement. A vortex of energy envelops you like wings of an angel. You feel the energy embracing you and radiating to you a divine awareness of your life's sacredness and holiness. You experience an intimacy and expansiveness simultaneously. You feel your spirit soaring in oneness with a spiral of light. It is a spiral dance of light and life.

Like the center of a labyrinth, the powerful vesica piscis speaks to your soul in a light language of mystical union. Your senses merge with the source of all and a profound evolved sensitivity emerges. Your eyes now absorb the vibration, the music of the spheres. You are attuned to the infinite. You radiate with the energies of awe and wonderment.

As the pulsating light stimulates the flow of energies in your kundalini you have a sense of your life expression being a channel of inspiration for others just as there are those in spirit channeling inspiration to you. You sense that the points of light of the mandala are benefactors in spirit—angels and loved ones—who offer support, protection, guidance, and direction. You are filled with awareness that you are sustained by invisible support and love. You experience the profoundness of eternal togetherness.

As you draw your attention back from the mandala, you have a sensing that you have experienced an awakening of your divine being. You are aware of a "brightening" in your spirit, a brilliance to your soul. You are filled with an unshakable faith in knowing you are attuned with all of life. The mandala now takes on the image of a roadmap/lifemap to peace and understanding, a map that you can revisit whenever you feel the inner calling to bask in the light of eternal freedom and warm your soul.

Part Two

Becoming a Vibrational Match to Your Desires

Hearts in my mind
Hearts of the soul
Hearts that will
Never fold
Hearts like the sea
Wide and vast
Ever widening
Ever steadfast

—J. R. Oyler

Chapter Four
Essentials for Attracting Love

Begin where you are. Begin now.
—Norman Vincent Peale

Awakening to Your Dreams

Going down a one-way street the wrong way? Passing your dreams along the way? Most of us continue down the same old path a very long time before we become aware that we are not happy. We work hard, struggle, and take repetitive steps that keep us in the same spiritual and emotional location. We ignore many signs along the way directing us toward happiness. Sometimes neon lights flash before us that read DEAD END or TAKE ANOTHER PATH, but we often choose not to see these flashes of light, or we choose to interpret them as meaningless or perhaps meant for someone else. We get comfortable with our pain, and more often than not, being comfortable prevents us from taking an unknown road that brings us closer to our heart's desires.

55

How many of us notice the amount of time we spend talking about our problems, heartaches, and unfulfilled dreams? How many of us energize what is going wrong in our lives by venting to numerous people about our disappointments in our work, our relationships, our children? How many of us choose to see ourselves as victims?

Changing the direction of our life happens when we decide to read the signs along the road and make a decision to pay attention to what these signs (our soul's guidance) are saying. We awaken to our dreams by thoughtfully placing each foot in front of the other one. Each step forward is movement within a sacred journey, a road that has only one name on it, your name. No one can walk this path for you. If you choose not to take it, it will be left unwalked, waiting for you to become ready in this lifetime, or perhaps in another. Why not start the journey now?

UNIVERSAL LAWS

> *A loving person lives in a loving world.*
> *A hostile person lives in a hostile world.*
> *Everyone you meet is your mirror.*
> —Ken Keyes, Jr., *Handbook to Higher Consciousness*

Law of Attraction

The Law of Attraction is the basis of the entire Universe. The Law of Attraction can be defined as: vibrations of similar frequencies that are magnetized to each other. In essence, one's thought draws in other thoughts of a similar vibration.

Simply put, we attract what we give attention to, or what we focus on. If we focus our thoughts on our desires, we can attract them. However, if we focus on not having what we want, we will create obstructions that repel our desires. Beliefs are patterns of thought. We attract experiences that are in alignment with our beliefs. For example, if we desire a loving intimate relationship, but we believe we are unworthy or have little to offer to a potential mate, then a satisfying relationship will not be forthcoming.

When I was in graduate school I did research on the psychological well-being of individuals experiencing domestic violence. While psychologists have known for a long time that our level of self-esteem affects the kind of relationships we bring into our experiences, the Law of Attraction clarifies this even further.

In general, the results of the interviews with individuals who were abused demonstrated they did not value themselves. Many of them had self-deprecating thoughts, such as, "I am not attractive," or "I am not a good lover," or "I am not a good mother." These beliefs, while not true, were a strong message to the Universe about what they felt worthy to receive. Whatever we believe about ourselves will be affirmed through the Law of Attraction. Thus, these individuals attracted abusers who affirmed over and over again their greatest belief about themselves: that they were not worthy of love and respect.

The Law of Attraction, just like the Law of Gravity, is an invisible energy force. While we cannot see gravity, we can see the results of it as our feet are planted firmly on the ground. Neither can we see the Law of Attraction, but we can see the results of it as we correlate our thoughts, feelings, and beliefs with the experiences we are creating.

THE ROLE OF EMOTIONS

Emotions create a vibration that moves our thoughts and desires throughout the Universe. The stronger the emotion, the more powerful the movement through space and time, attracting whatever we are giving our attention to, in that moment. The stronger the emotion—positive or negative—the more quickly our thoughts create our experiences.

Our thoughts can be focused in one of two directions—the intention of having something we desire or the fear of not having it. It is difficult to monitor our thoughts because they come so quickly into our mind. It is much easier to pay attention to our emotions. Our emotions provide guidance to us with regard to the direction of our thoughts. When our emotions are positive, our thoughts are in alignment with our desires. When our emotions are negative, our thoughts are not in alignment with our desires. Whatever we focus our thoughts on is what we attract into our experience.

For instance, when I was dating Ron, we went through a difficult period in our relationship when it looked like it might end. I feared that everything might fall apart, and I gave a great deal of attention to the "what ifs" of our relationship not continuing. At that time I did not understand the Law of Attraction or I would have known that I was sabotaging my own desires. Had I paid attention to the negative emotion I felt when I focused attention on the possibility of breaking up, I would have been guided to redirect my thoughts toward my desire of staying together. Alternatively, I could have focused my attention on working through our disagreements and creating a harmonious relationship. These thoughts would have allowed me to become a vibrational match for my desires, and if it had been in our highest good, we might have stayed together. I did not do this, and eventually our relationship ended.

Law of Allowing

The Law of Allowing can be defined as: acceptance of what you or others have attracted without any resistance. It is different from tolerating, which is "putting up with" something that displeases us. Tolerating always creates negative emotion within us. "Allowing" always creates positive emotion within us.

A person who understands and lives by the Law of Allowing rather than tolerating is called an allower. An allower is free from negative thoughts, including judgment, fear, anger, and resentment. An allower feels great love and compassion for himself and others, but understands that all of us are creators of our experience.

All situations, wanted and unwanted, have been attracted through our vibration and have value to us. As allowers we will ask ourselves the question: What new desire has evolved from this situation? Unwanted situations can be transcended, once we shift the direction of our thoughts toward the desire, releasing negative emotion associated with what we originally attracted, and replacing it with positive emotion. Unwanted experiences can enhance the strength of the new desire when our thoughts are positively focused.

For instance, at one point in my life I dated a man who defined the world in terms of right or wrong, good or bad. When we did not see eye to eye, he would launch into a long-winded monologue, justifying why he was right and I was wrong. This became tiring, and after countless discussions with no sign of relief in sight, I ended the relationship. The clear and powerful new desire that was born within me was to attract an intimate relationship with a man who was open-minded, and who could engage in harmonious and respectful discussions when disagreements occurred.

We attract pain and suffering because of the way we view our life circumstances. When we determine that something or someone is right or wrong, good or bad, we are engaging in the process of judging. When we judge ourselves or others, we create, through the Law of Attraction, more opportunities to be judged, thus embarking on an endless cycle of pain and suffering.

For example, if you have chosen a vegetarian lifestyle, as I have, because of your spiritual beliefs, you can choose to tolerate or allow the opinions of other people on the subject. If you determine that other people are wrong in their choice, then you are making a judgment, and, therefore, tolerating the decision they have made, rather than allowing it. Tolerating is judgment, and it attracts others judging us. In addition, tolerating creates more of what we do not want by sending a low vibratory signal into the Universe.

As we tolerate, or "put up with" the choices of others, we create a struggle within us, resulting in negative emotion. Anything we struggle with, or fight against, binds us to the source of our discontent, causing us to attract more and more of the things we are resisting. The stronger the resistance, the more we energize what we do not want by giving attention to it. In addition, the negative emotion created from the struggle lowers our vibration and inhibits us from attracting our desires.

A better option would be to allow others the freedom to make their choices without making them wrong or judging them. Allowing frees our energy so we are not defending our position, or fighting against someone else. Freeing our energy allows us to expand and have a greater impact on the world. Unlike tolerating, allowing someone to make decisions that are different from our own creates positive emotion, because you are trusting in, and therefore energizing, the well-being of all concerned. For example, I can energize the well-being of animals by being *for* the ethical treatment of them rather than *against* cruelty. Being *for* your desire creates a high vibration and therefore has a positive impact in the world. Being *against* someone or something has a low frequency, and attracts obstructions to attaining your desire.

What most people do not realize is that the things we struggle with, fight against, or protect get energized, and become our experience. In our resistance, we focus our attention on what we do not want. This creates a similar vibration to whatever we are struggling with, or fighting against. Until resistance is replaced with allowing, the Law of Attraction will bring us endless opportunities to release the struggle and align our vibration with love. We can spend our entire life in a struggle mode, or we can tune into love and create a joyous existence. It is our choice.

Put the Past Behind You

> *Dwell not on the past.*
> *Use it to illustrate a point, then leave it*
> *behind. Nothing really matters except what*
> *you do now in this instant of time.*
> *From this moment onward you can be an*
> *entirely different person, filled with love and*
> *understanding, ready with an outstretched*
> *hand, uplifted and positive in every thought*
> *and deed.*
>
> —Eileen Caddy, *God Spoke to Me*

Many of us hold onto unresolved and painful experiences. My friend, Joan Duhaime, calls this "filling our pockets with stuff," those painful memories filled with self-doubt and frustration. The Universe "highlights" these unresolved issues through the Law of Attraction, which ensures that similar experiences continue to come into our life until we create thoughts that feel better to us.

The word "highlight" is a good description of the process. Imagine an intense light shining on an object in the road as you are traveling by car late one night. The light allows you to see the object so you can make a decision about how to approach it. Similarly, the Universe "brings to light" any unresolved and emotionally charged issue by giving us endless opportunities to see what is in front of us, and to replace pain and self-doubt with deeper levels of love. Alan Cohen calls this an "in-your-face production," because the original issue, unless dealt with, gets bigger and bigger until it is unavoidable.

Until we deal with our emotionally charged issues, we will relive pain and self-doubt, lowering our vibration, and ensuring that we attract more things to stuff in our pockets. This affects our level of happiness, because the more we stuff into our pockets, the less content we are with our lives.

Pocket Syndrome

Most people maintain a threshold for how much pain and how much happiness they allow into their life. When our level for happiness starts to shift out of our comfort zone, we unconsciously attract situations and circumstances that maintain this level. In addition, we unconsciously monitor our happiness level by how much we allow undesirable circumstances to affect us. By this I mean that the degree to which we allow things to upset us depends upon how many other pressing issues are stuffed in our pocket.

For instance, have you ever noticed how some days you handle a disagreement with ease, and other days you blow things out of proportion? Have you noticed that when things are going well in one area of your life, another area seems to be out of whack? For example, you finally get your personal life in balance, and now the relationship with your business partner is filled with tension. This is the "pocket syndrome."

We unconsciously define how much good we allow ourselves to receive, and the Universe responds by affirming our beliefs about ourselves through the Law of Attraction. Our comfort zone for happiness reflects how much we think we deserve in life. The more happiness we allow into our life, the more deeply we love ourselves. The more we love ourselves, the greater our capacity to love others, and the greater our capability to receive genuine love. Self-love is the foundation for attracting a loving relationship, or for that matter, any other desire.

Take Christina, for instance. She has experienced a strained relationship with her boss for many years. Now she is happy at work for the first time in a long time. She just got a new boss and they are in the honeymoon phase of their relationship. Until recently, her long-term intimate relationship with Ted was going very well and he was always supportive of her ups and downs at work. She could talk to Ted about anything and know that he was there for her. Now, just when things are going great in her career, Ted announces that he needs time away from the relationship and more time with his male friends. Christina is wondering if he has lost interest in her. She is pondering thoughts like, Perhaps Ted has met another woman and is having an affair. After all, he hasn't paid much attention to her lately, and he doesn't do those little things he used to do, like write love notes and leave them throughout their apartment. In actuality, Ted still loves Christina, and plans to remain faithful to the relationship.

Notice how Christina's pocket was originally filled with concerns about her relationship with her boss. Now with her new boss, those feelings are gone. Christina became a vibrational match for her desires at work, and attracted a new and satisfying experience for herself.

However, what Christina did not do, and this is very important, is set the intention for higher levels of joy in all areas of her life (more about setting intentions in chapter 6). By not doing this, her overall level for happiness remained the same. As we set intentions to feel higher levels of joy in our life, we will consciously begin the process of emptying the contents of our pockets, rather than juggling them.

The diagrams in exhibit B demonstrate this concept.

What's in Your Pockets?

It is time to examine the contents of your pockets. Below is a sampling of "pocket stuffers." Any of these items can completely fill your pocket for as long as you allow it, holding you back from the happiness that awaits you. One item alone, if you dwell on it, can completely consume you, keeping you at a lower vibration and preventing you from becoming a vibrational match to your desirable relationship.

Let's take a peek at some of the things you might have inside your pockets. Answer the following questions with a simple yes or no:

Do I . . .
Have unresolved issues with family members, friends, past

Exhibit B   Pocket Syndrome

Diagram One

Pocket level before setting the intention for higher levels of joy in all areas of life:

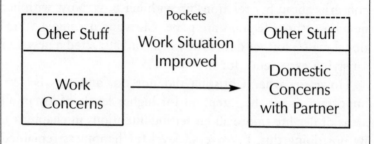

Pockets

Other Stuff

Work Concerns

Work Situation Improved →

Other Stuff

Domestic Concerns with Partner

Diagram Two

Pocket level after setting the intention for higher levels of joy in all areas of life:

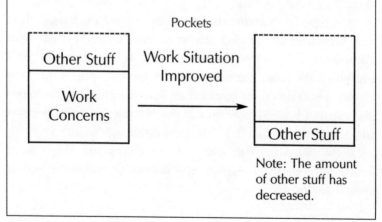

Pockets

Other Stuff

Work Concerns

Work Situation Improved →

Other Stuff

Note: The amount of other stuff has decreased.

lovers, or spouses that on average I think about at least once a week?

Vent about what I do not like about previous dates or intimate relationships?

Reference the opposite sex or previous dates as "jerks" or use some other negative comment to describe them?

Feel that I am unattractive, having thoughts like, I am too heavy, or too short, or too this or that?

Live with regrets and ongoing negative "self talk"?

Hold anger or grudges when family members, friends, or intimate relationships do not meet my expectations?

Keep what I perceive as "embarrassing moments" alive in my memory by rehashing them over and over again?

Feel emotionally and physically tired from conversations I have with myself about any aspect of my life?

Say yes when I mean to say no?

Say no when I mean to say yes?

Feel I must prove or justify myself to family, friends, co-workers, or my boss?

Tell "half truths" or lies?

Become silent when I have something I want to say?

Regularly spend time doing things I dread or resent?

Worry about what people think or whether or not people like me?

It Is Time to Empty Our Pockets

Okay, we have examined the contents of our pockets and we can see there are a number of unresolved issues that have accumulated over a period of time. We have unfinished business with an item when thinking about it triggers even the slightest negative emotion.

How can we release these nagging painful memories once and for all? The answer is to consciously change our thoughts about the issues. Just as a picture can look completely different when surrounded by various frames, the thoughts we create to "frame up" a relationship, situation, or circumstance in our lives make a significant difference in how we feel about ourselves. We can either build ourselves up or tear ourselves down, depending upon the thoughts that surround us. Building ourselves up at the expense of tearing someone else down will not raise our vibration, but will in fact lower it.

We can reframe a situation by purposefully creating the most positive and believable thought (although it may be a stretch) that feels good, and building upon it in the direction of our desires. Abraham-Hicks calls this "reaching for a better feeling thought." In order to do this you may need to change a belief about yourself, someone else, or about a situation.

For example: Once again Paul is in the middle of an argument with Jen over her being late. She was supposed to meet him at the restaurant at 6:00 P.M. and instead she shows up at 6:45, giving yet another excuse for her tardiness. Paul believes that Jen's behavior reflects a lack of caring for him, when in fact this is not true. Jen's tardiness has nothing to do with Paul, as she is late for everything. It has to do with her mismanagement of time. If Paul can see the situation for what it is, and not take it personally, he can raise his vibration and step out of this vicious cycle of arguing. As Paul maintains his cool he can have a rational discussion with Jen and establish parameters that work for both of them.

The reason we hold onto negative thoughts about ourselves or someone else is that we hold a belief that inhibits us from seeing the situation from a compassionate, loving perspective. In the example above, as Paul shifts his thoughts away from what he does not want to his new desire, he is raising his vibration and opening to a higher consciousness. As he raises his vibration, he will have access to thoughts that enable him to see the situation without judgment. Releasing criticism will free him from negativity, and he will be aligning with the Law of Allowing as he unfolds into a sense of well-being. Potential solutions will become obvious, and enable him to create a harmonious relationship with Jen, if this is what he truly desires.

WELL-BEING

> *Your natural state is that of well-being. Your natural state is one of health. Your world is abundant with all that you consider to be good, and you have easy access to that abundance.*
>
> —Abraham-Hicks

Our overall vibration is reflective of our mental and emotional state of being, which is the foundation from which we attract our desires. The greater our self-esteem, the higher our vibration and the stronger our foundation from which to launch our desires. When we do not value ourselves, we attract more of the things we do not want. For example:

1. We cannot attract love if we are feeling unlovable; instead, we will attract more reasons to feel rejected.
2. We cannot attract happiness if we are feeling unhappy; instead, we will attract experiences aligned with our concept of sadness.
3. We cannot attract prosperity if we are feeling poor; instead, we will attract more reasons to feel financially insecure.
4. We cannot attract a desirable companion if we are feeling unattractive; instead, we will attract more reasons to feel unsatisfied with ourselves.
5. We cannot feel in charge of our life if we are feeling like a victim; instead, we will attract more reasons to feel that our life is out of control.
6. We cannot attract abundance if we are focused on scarcity; instead, we will attract more reasons to feel that we do not have enough of whatever we desire.

In order for our energy to flow, it is important to minimize resistance to our desires. When we allow our natural state of well-being, we are aligned with the Universe and our energy flows. When we are anxious, fearful, or feeling any negative emotion, we are holding on to our old way of thinking about a particular subject or person. Thoughts that create negative emotions often get buried and eat away at us. We must reframe our thoughts in order to see them from a higher perspective, thus creating positive feelings. Shifting to a positive viewpoint allows us to release and therefore complete whatever was left undone. Essentially, this is what forgiveness is all about and why it is so very important. When we forgive ourselves or someone else, we are choosing to release our judgments and in so doing we are choosing to feel good rather than bad, positive rather than negative, free rather than imprisoned.

Many of us tend to repeat the same patterns throughout our lives. At some point in our early years of living we probably experienced the feeling of inadequacy. Most of us did not know how to restructure our thoughts to create positive feelings about ourselves. Most likely, we buried our feelings of inadequacy and harbored anger toward ourselves and others. If the thoughts that triggered these feelings were never dealt with, they have remained with us. They rise again and again when we least expect it, attracting more opportunities to feel inadequate. Once we learn to reframe our thoughts, we will attract people and circumstances that are in alignment with our thinking. Reframing our thoughts into something positive will stimulate positive feelings. If we are ever in doubt about where we are standing in terms of our thoughts and feelings about unfinished business, all we need to do is look around at our immediate life experience. The Universe always reflects a perfect picture of our consciousness. If we focus our energy on restructuring our thoughts about our present life situation, we will be addressing significant unfinished business from the past, without necessarily having to reenergize our childhood traumas.

Nurturing ourselves will make us resilient, like a flower. If a flower is not planted firmly in the soil, it will be uprooted by the wind. If a flower is not watered, it will wither away in hot weather. We are no different from the beautiful flower. We must nurture ourselves by paying attention to our feelings and our desires. We must make a conscious decision to release negative thoughts and create thoughts that bring forth positive emotion. We must believe in the goodness of ourselves and other people. Through this effort we will truly know peace and understand that our life is in perfect order. We will experience the abundance of the Universe, and know without a doubt that all is well.

GRATITUDE

> *Gratitude is the acknowledgment of love and well-being. It is a state of mind that creates a direct pathway between ourselves and the abundance of the Universe.*
> —Margaret McCraw

Gratitude is a state of mind. It creates a very high vibration that energizes our desires. When we are in a state of gratitude we are open to seeing the gifts around us and to receiving them as well. Our thoughts are optimistic and we are inspired to take risks that normally we would not consider. Gratitude allows us to see that "problems" are not really problems but simply incorrect thinking about a situation. Being in a state of gratitude energizes more and more things to be grateful for. Anything we do for someone else always uplifts the giver as much as or more than the receiver, for all gifts are multiplied and returned to the giver.

When we give from our heart, we are in a state of gratitude. Gratitude is the acknowledgment of love and well-being. This is the state of mind in which we create and give birth to new ventures. For in this state of mind, we are creating a direct pathway between ourselves and the abundance of the

Universe. We are allowing all the goodness around us to enter into our experience, and we are saying yes to all that we desire.

Our state of mind will be healthy if we can maintain a sense of gratitude throughout each day. We will be uplifted by the little things in life and in this high, pure vibration we will attract more and more things that please us.

WHOLENESS

If you know your true worth, you do not need anyone else to confirm it. If you do not recognize your value, you will not gain it by getting others to approve.

—Alan Cohen

Wholeness is about love, or viewing ourselves and others without judgment. Acknowledging our wholeness is the process of emotional healing. Emotional healing involves looking at yourself with loving eyes. It is a journey that lasts a lifetime, filled with peaks and valleys as you look into your soul, growing in love with yourself on deeper levels.

There are no limits to love, so there can be no end points to the ebb and flow of emotional healing. Healing always involves shifting our thoughts so that we release judgment of ourselves or others. It is an ongoing process of self-discovery as we evolve into the purest vibration of light, aligning with the highest consciousness in the Universe.

Our relationships, particularly our intimate connections, serve to deepen our self-love as they reveal areas within us that can benefit from healing. As healing occurs we acknowledge our wholeness, growing deeper and deeper in love with ourselves. It is only through self-love that we can truly love others, and as we love others we expand the love we have for ourselves. Love is cyclical in nature.

LOVE YOURSELF

> *I have an everyday religion that works for me. Love yourself first and everything else falls into line.*
>
> —Lucille Ball

Self-love is experienced as joy. Joy is a deep inner feeling of well-being. There is a direct correlation between the depth of self-love and the amount of joy we feel in our life. A joyous relationship is one in which each person brings to the table a deep level of self-love, and the couple basks in the brightness of the light they emanate.

Many of us are under the illusion that romantic relationships will bring us true joy. However, joy is never found through anything or anyone outside of ourselves. We experience joy with another person as a reflection of our own sense of well-being. Well-being is present regardless of the circumstances around us. Our ability to realize this is directly related to the depth of self-love we have allowed.

If we have not cultivated our own sense of well-being, the feeling of euphoria so commonly experienced in a new relationship often fades into disillusionment. This is why marriages all too frequently dissolve into divorce, with individuals experiencing further disappointment in relationships that follow.

Until we are willing to go deep within ourselves, releasing judgments and replacing them with love, we will create an endless cycle of unmet expectations. Attracting happiness is always correlated with the level of worth or love we have for ourselves. As we learn to set intentions for happiness (chapter 7), we will attract opportunities for emotional healing. Allowing these opportunities to unfold lovingly is the path to creating a joyous relationship.

LIVING FROM THE HIGHEST
DEGREE OF INTEGRITY

> *It's a funny thing about life; if you accept*
> *anything but the very best, you will get it.*
> —W. Somerset Maugham

During one of my meditations, I was guided to make all my decisions using the 100 percent rule. Simply, the 100 percent rule states that if something feels 100 percent right, say yes, and anything less than 100 percent, say no. The message conveyed to me was that I am worthy of living a life (as is everyone) that is in total alignment with my desires, and that the Universe would completely support me in making decisions that felt totally right for me. If I made decisions that felt 50 percent acceptable to me, the Universe would also support me. However, why make half-hearted decisions when you know you can have it all?

When I first started dating John, I thought he was that one special guy I would commit to forever. I enjoyed his company and we had a lot in common. I loved our time together and we bonded intellectually, emotionally, and physically. However, we were not spiritually compatible. I could not talk to John about my beliefs without it upsetting him, as he wanted me to "fit into" the church he attended. I knew this would never happen. I very much desired a strong spiritual bond with an intimate partner, and it was clear that I would not have this with him. Good friends encouraged me to "hang in there" because the relationship had 75 percent of what I was looking for (emotional, intellectual, and physical bonding), but I knew this did not feel right. When I made the decision to end the relationship, I felt relief. I was coming from a place of integrity, and this always feels good. When I decided to tell John that I wanted to shift our relationship to a platonic friendship, he felt relief too. Clearly, he wanted a spiritual bond with a partner as much as I did, and both of us knew our beliefs were incompatible, and that we could not offer this to each other.

Sometimes when we review our options, nothing feels 100 percent right, yet we are faced with making a decision. If we are feeling at all anxious about a pending decision, we may not be seeing all of our options, as fear has a way of creeping in and blinding us. The best way to handle this is to set the intention to make a decision that is 100 percent aligned with our highest good, and to ask the Universe to bring absolute clarity to us so we will know without a doubt how to proceed. We must try to relax and be patient while paying attention to the messages that appear in our meditations, dreams, or through some other source.

There is no right or wrong answer, or a logical set of rules to follow that can be applied to every circumstance. However, there is a guiding principle that simply involves asking ourselves what feels right and true to our heart in each situation.

We are all worthy of living a life that is of the highest degree of integrity. If we believe this, we will make decisions that are 100 percent aligned with who we are. In doing this, the Law of Attraction will work for us and the Universe will support us fully in the choices we make for ourselves. Decisions that are not within the highest degree of integrity will be accompanied by negative emotion. For example, when a decision feels like a sacrifice, we are not in alignment with our true self. Sacrificing leads to resentment and creates negative feelings. Sacrifices are made by individuals who do not believe they can have it all. Sacrifices are indicative of a scarcity consciousness. However, when we give freely from our heart, the emotion we feel is positive. Giving rather than sacrificing keeps us tuned into the abundance of the Universe. Aligning with the belief of abundance means making choices that feel 100 percent right to us 100 percent of the time.

Chapter Five

Frequency One: Create "Feel-Good" Moments

Be like a very small joyous child living glori-
ously in the ever present Now without a sin-
gle worry or concern about even the next
moment of time.

—Eileen Caddy

There are four frequencies to a successful connection that include:

1. create feel-good moments
2. identify your desires
3. activate your intentions
4. release the outcome

Each frequency builds upon the other and can be visually seen in exhibit C. The more you understand the components that make up each frequency, the more easily and quickly you will manifest your desires.

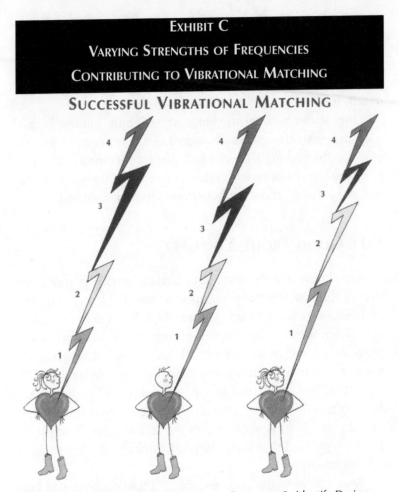

SUCCESSFUL VIBRATIONAL MATCHING

Frequency 1: Create Feel-Good Moments   Frequency 2: Identify Desires
Frequency 3: Activate Intentions   Frequency 4: Release Outcome

All three individuals have successfully become
a vibrational match to their desire; however, the impact
of each frequency varied in each case.

FOCUS ON GOOD MEMORIES

Everyone possesses a storehouse of special moments that
qualify as his or her unique "watercolored" memories. What

are yours? Do you remember your feelings of triumph and pride on graduation day? Or the blissful feeling that spread over you when you were kissed by someone special? Will you ever forget how happy you felt when you attracted that dream job?

One of the wonderful things about being human is that we can revisit those special moments whenever we wish. In addition to making us feel good, happy memories have the extraordinary ability to elevate our energy levels, increase our self-esteem, and even boost our immune systems!

FEEL GOOD ABOUT YOURSELF

Rose knew that she wanted to attract a loving partner, but she was haunted by her perception of past failures. "Skip, my ex-husband, told me I was great in bed, but a zero as a partner. When we divorced, he told me no one would want a 35-year-old woman who "couldn't keep a job." She sighed. "I guess my chances of finding someone are one in a million."

Debra, her vibrational match counselor, had to agree that Rose certainly wouldn't attract the type of man she desired as long as she was radiating negative thoughts. Therefore, Debra suggested that Rose shift her thinking to a more positive vibration.

Rose was intrigued, but skeptical. "How on earth can I do that?" she asked. Debra had Rose select three activities that she enjoyed. Rose quickly came up with, "Well, I love petting my cat and playing with my dog. Does that sound silly?" Debra reassured her that whatever made her feel good was exactly what she needed to think about, and imagine doing.

"I'm also very good at counseling my friends," Rose continued, her voice a bit stronger now. "I get at least three calls a day from friends who need advice. They say I'm their friendly neighborhood psychologist."

"That's two," agreed her counselor. "Got a third?"

"Well," mused Rose, "I love playing the piano. My daughter sings along with me and we always have a lot of fun."

Debra nodded. "Rose, now I'd like you to choose one of those three positive experiences and focus on *how you felt at the moment it was happening.*"

Rose immediately selected the day her best friend said, "I don't know what I'd do without you," after Rose had offered her some excellent advice. Rose glowed as she shared how important that moment had been for her, and her counselor used this "feel-good moment" to help Rose move toward vibrating at a stronger, more positive frequency.

Then, Debra took her through her other two "feel-good" moments, observing, as they relived each one, how Rose's appearance began to change. Her sad, dull eyes became warm and bright, her tense face relaxed into a gentle smile, and even her posture straightened as she relived her "water-colored" memories.

Now it was time to reinforce the new, higher vibration Rose had begun to generate. Her counselor suggested that Rose close her eyes and imagine she was on her way to a place of her own choosing where she would feel a deep sense of inner peace. Rose immediately chose a beach she had visited years ago in the Bahamas. "It was so peaceful, I just wanted to stay there forever."

As Debra took Rose on a guided journey to the beach, the last vestige of her earlier negativity disappeared, and she was smiling as she saw herself sitting on the beach watching dolphins leaping in the waters, the glorious sun shining on her body.

By the time her journey was completed, Rose was imbued with the most loving thoughts about herself and her life. She was now ready to move up the vibrational ladder to Frequency Two.

Before moving on to the next frequency, let's reflect on how our emotions help us monitor our thoughts.

GREEN, YELLOW, AND RED

Green Light—Continue Thinking as You Are

Your feelings are very important indicators of how close you are to connecting with a vibration that will bring you whatever you desire. When you feel good about yourself and life, as Rose did after her journey to the beach, your "Feeling Indicator Light" is a bright green. This tells you that you are on course to "Go!" If you continue thinking as you are, you will be able to ride the manifestation vibration in the direction of your desires.

Yellow Light—Slow Down and Pay Attention!

When you are feeling unsettled or unfocused, your thoughts are only partially aligned with your wishes. In this case, your "Feeling Indicator Light" is yellow. Tell yourself to "slow down" when you are not feeling clear or positive.

So how can you get off this self-defeating frequency? Simply distract yourself by shifting your thoughts to a more positive subject. This will help you move out of a place of deprivation and into an appreciation mode, which always raises your vibration to a higher level. Once thoughts of "I can't do it" or "I'm worthless" are replaced with "I'm capable" and "I'm worthy," a shift will take place in the physical as well as mental and emotional bodies. Now is the time to consciously become more optimistic.

Red Light—Stop and Shift the Direction of Your Thoughts!

When you are feeling unhappy, your thoughts are definitely out of alignment with your desires, and your "Feeling Indicator Light" is now red. Positive creativity is at a standstill, and your attention is focused on what you *do not* want. When your vibration is low, it is difficult to attract good things into your life, for, as you know, "like attracts like."

Review exhibit D for a better understanding of how to use your "Feeling Indicator Light" to align your thoughts with your desires.

Frequency One: Create "Feel-Good" Moments

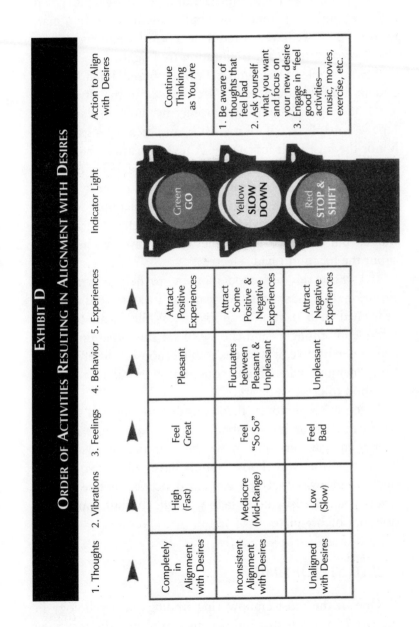

EXHIBIT D

ORDER OF ACTIVITIES RESULTING IN ALIGNMENT WITH DESIRES

1. Thoughts	2. Vibrations	3. Feelings	4. Behavior	5. Experiences	Indicator Light	Action to Align with Desires
Completely in Alignment with Desires	High (Fast)	Feel Great	Pleasant	Attract Positive Experiences	Green GO	Continue Thinking as You Are
Inconsistent Alignment with Desires	Mediocre (Mid-Range)	Feel "So So"	Fluctuates between Pleasant & Unpleasant	Attract Some Positive & Negative Experiences	Yellow SLOW DOWN	1. Be aware of thoughts that feel bad 2. Ask yourself what you want and focus on your new desire 3. Engage in "feel good" activities—music, movies, exercise, etc.
Unaligned with Desires	Low (Slow)	Feel Bad	Unpleasant	Attract Negative Experiences	Red STOP & SHIFT	

Many times we begin thinking of a pleasant memory and then we remember something unpleasant about it. In a matter of seconds we have shifted from a positive and high vibration (green light) to a low vibration (red light).

For example, I remember how enthused I felt when I bought my first house, which was located in the city. I have good memories about decorating my house, planting a Japanese maple tree with my sister, and creating a garden to honor the love I felt for nature. A few days after I moved in, a friend stopped by and elaborated on the dangers of living in the city. She made it clear that she would never live in the location I had selected, and that she was planning to buy a home in the suburbs where she felt safe. By the time she walked out the door I was questioning my own judgment about the location I had selected.

If I chose this feel-good moment to help me raise my vibration, I might shift from warm and fuzzy to cold and disheartened in a matter of moments. While I can certainly reframe my thoughts and choose to see this situation from a higher perspective, it is just as well to choose a different feel-good memory when I am consciously trying to raise my vibration to create a desire.

If you are a pet lover, then consider holding and stroking your cat, dog, or house rabbit, as they exude pure positive energy and can very quickly soothe us into a pure vibration. No matter what you choose, simply have one or two memories tucked away that you can easily access, or one or two things you can easily do to help you quickly shift your vibration to a higher place.

CULTIVATE OPTIMISM

One of the most empowering findings in psychology in the last 25 years is that individuals can *choose* the *way* they think. The power of optimism has been well documented by

Dr. Martin Seligman, author of *Learned Optimism*, whose research confirmed that an optimistic attitude has a significant impact on longevity, success in aptitude tests, success in school, and success at work.

In brief, when we are feeling pessimistic we take undesirable events and blow them out of proportion, taking the blame or blaming others for the outcome. On the other hand, when we are feeling optimistic, we minimize the impact of undesirable events and focus our attention on what we can learn from the experience. Every experience is valued as one from which positive changes can be made to ensure more desirable results in the future. When we consciously choose to live from an optimistic perspective our vibration remains strong regardless of outside events, thus ensuring a higher degree of success in achieving a positive outcome for any situation.

Try the exercise below to determine if your current thought pattern *enhances* your vibration *or inhibits* you from creating your desirable match.

DO YOUR THOUGHTS TEND TO ENHANCE OR INHIBIT A DESIRABLE MATCH?

Rate each item (1–5) using the scale below. Which thought pattern do you use most frequently?

Number 1 indicates Never
Number 2 indicates Rarely
Number 3 indicates Sometimes
Number 4 indicates Frequently
Number 5 indicates All the Time

How often do you:

1. Respond to stressful situations with compassion rather than with judgement?
Rating (1–5)_____

2. Check in with others involved in a difficult situation rather than make negative assumptions?

Rating (1–5)_____

3. Step back from a difficult situation and be an observer rather than blow things out of proportion?

Rating (1–5)_____

4. Perceive situations as unique, rather than black and white or right and wrong?

Rating (1–5)_____

5. Set intentions to feel inner peace and harmony, rather than replay the same negative tapes in your head?

Rating (1–5)_____

6. Choose to focus attention on the good things happening in your life, rather than magnify the things that don't feel good?

Rating (1–5)_____

7. Maximize your strengths by being grateful for your personal gifts, rather than minimize your good qualities by putting yourself down?

Rating (1–5)_____

8. Detach from your emotions about difficult situations that you could take personally, rather than get angry?

Rating (1–5)_____

9. Focus on the positive qualities of people who do not easily agree with you, as well as situations that do not easily agree with you?

Rating (1–5)_____

10. Continue to have positive expectations regardless of a few undesirable experiences (e.g., "He is usually on time—this was an exception.")?

Rating (1–5)_____

11. Learn from an undesirable situation rather than blame self or others?

Rating (1–5)_____

12. Look for the gifts in unexpected situations rather than fearing the worst?

Rating (1–5)_____

13. Gather complete information about a situation rather than take statements or events out of context?

Rating (1–5)_____

14. Replace "should," "must," and "ought" statements (eliminating options) with "could," "might consider," "perhaps" statements (creating options)?

Rating (1–5)_____

15. Replace "need" statements with "desire" statements (shifting from must have or desperation to having a preference)?

Rating (1–5)_____

Score Yourself:

71–75 = Extremely Enhancing
61–70 = Very Enhancing
51–60 = Usually Enhancing
40–50 = Middle Ground—Sometimes Enhancing and
            Sometimes Inhibiting
30–39 = Usually Inhibiting
20–29 = Very Inhibiting
15–19 = Extremely Inhibiting

Regardless of your score, cultivating an optimistic perspective in all areas of your life will enhance your ability to attract your desirable vibrational match. The more positive our thoughts, the more quickly our desires are manifested. Review exhibits E and F to understand this concept better.

Since our thoughts come so quickly, it is much easier to monitor our feelings rather than our thoughts. Feelings are an indicator of the *direction* of our thoughts. Pay attention to your emotions and when you feel down, be willing to shift your thoughts to a higher perspective. In doing this you will elevate your vibration, enabling your desires to be drawn into your experience.

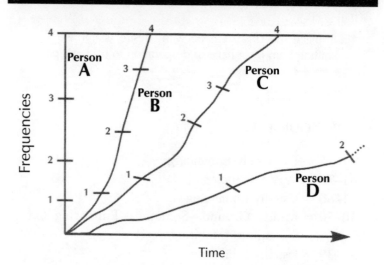

EXHIBIT E

IMPACT OF INHIBITORS* ON

VIBRATIONAL MATCHING

A: Zero Resistance in each frequency level resulting in instantaneous manifestation.

B: Minor Resistance in each frequency level resulting in some time delay in manifestation.

C: Moderate Resistance in each frequency level resulting in a moderate time delay in manifestation.

D: Great Resistance in each frequency level resulting in a great time delay in manifestation.

* Inhibitors = Resistance: What We Fear, Worry About, Defend Against, Prepare Against, or Struggle With

WHAT YOU RESIST—YOU ATTRACT!!

EXHIBIT F

IMPACT OF ENHANCERS & INHIBITORS
AND LOVING YOURSELF ON VIBRATIONAL MATCHING

*All of us have the ability to enhance or inhibit manifestation of our desires.
Enhancers will accelerate the progress while inhibitors slow it down.
Loving yourself is the primary source for creating your desired relationship.
The process is cyclical in that successful vibrational matching
also increases the sense of self-worth.*

SUCCESSFUL VIBRATIONAL MATCHING

ENHANCERS *Create Positive Emotion*		INHIBITORS *Create Negative Emotion*
Optimism about present life circumstances	RELEASE OUTCOME (Frequency 4)	Pessimism about present life circumstances
Strong desire and strong belief in your ability to manifest what you want	ACTIVATE INTENTIONS (Frequency 3)	Minimal desire and belief in your ability to manifest what you want
Attention on what you desire	IDENTIFY DESIRE (Frequency 2)	Attention on what you don't have
Attention on things that feel good	FEEL GOOD (Frequency 1)	Attention on things that feel bad

LOVING YOURSELF
The Energy Source of All Successful Vibrational Matching

Tune into Love

"Getting high" about yourself and the life you are creating is more than a "feel-good" process. It is the first step towards attracting the partnership you have always desired. Do you deserve to have your dreams come true? Of course you do!

I feel your heart beat
Your breath on my neck
The soft feel of your lips

My invisible lover
Heart of my desire

Come to me

I am yours
You are mine
            —Sherry Tuegel

FREQUENCY ONE: LOVE BOOSTERS

Create Feel-Good Moments

Choose your favorite or do them all.

- Go to a special place outdoors and enjoy a picnic lunch.
- Enjoy a sport? Go play! Increase your endorphins.
- Spend time with pets—yours or someone else's.
- Get some crayons and draw a happy picture—sunshine, flowers, and trees. Put yourself in the picture!
- Listen to some upbeat music.
- Grab your camera and go on a photo shoot. Be sure and get someone to take your picture while you are doing something fun.
- Pick up a funny movie and some popcorn and invite your favorite person to join you for a chuckle.
- Call a friend who uplifts you. Have a good laugh together.
- Go to a playground and watch children have fun. Try out the monkey bars, the seesaw, and the swing. Don't go home until you have done it all.
- Pick up some flowers for someone you know will enjoy them—that person might be you!
- Plant a seed in a cup like you did in kindergarten. Be sure and give it plenty of water and sunshine, and every day watch it grow.
- Pick up the telephone and tell someone you love them "with all your heart and soul." Look in a mirror and tell yourself the same thing.
- Wake up every day and say with all the gusto you can muster, "*I Am Joy, I Am Love, and I Am Light.* It is my intention to uplift everyone I come into contact with today and every day."
- Draw a big heart on a piece of paper. Write your name in the middle of the heart and then around it, create a free-flowing gratitude list. Keep adding to it daily.

FREQUENCY ONE AT-A-GLANCE REFERENCE GUIDE

- Lighten up! Be playful. Be grateful. Have fun with this process in co-creation.

- Create a light-hearted mood as often as possible. Laugh frequently and smile at others. Find things that bring a smile to your face and frequently re-create this mental picture for yourself, e.g., children playing.

- As often as possible do things that bring forth the feeling of contentment: playing with a pet, watching a comedy, reading a good book, taking a walk, exercising, taking a hot bath, surrounding yourself with flowers. Many of these things do not require much time or money.

- When thoughts creep in that feel less than good, consciously and quickly shift your attention to something else more uplifting. Distraction is a very good technique, so have some easy and readily available things you can focus your attention on whether you are at home, in the office, or driving your car.

- Create opportunities to uplift someone else. Call someone's boss and tell them what great service was offered to you. Take extra time to help someone needing assistance or searching for a solution to a concern, etc.

- Develop the skill of changing your thinking patterns to a higher vibration by focusing on the positive qualities of yourself, others, or situations. Put love around everyone and everything by releasing shoulds, ought to's, must do's, issues, judgments, blame, assumptions, black/white and right/wrong thinking patterns. Instead, practice the art of allowing yourself and others to attract experiences without labeling the outcome as good or bad, right or wrong.

- Daydream often about your accomplishments and desires.

- Be grateful, for this is the energy that creates miracles. Gratitude will attract abundance and joy into your life. Keep a running gratitude list on paper and in your mind and add to it daily. Remember to add things like the

rain, sunshine, flowers, pets, your friends and family,
etc. As you expand your list the Law of Attraction will
ensure you attract more and more things in your life to
appreciate.

• Take time each day to close your eyes and quiet your
mind. Listen rather than talk. Relax rather than think. Just
breathe deeply and allow thoughts and images from
source energy to be impressed on your mind. Fully allow
yourself to bathe in this unconditional love as you absorb
warmth, light, images, and messages.

Chapter Six
Frequency Two: Identify Your Desires

All things are possible under Divine Law.
—Eric Butterworth

USE YOUR IMAGINATION

Unless you can imagine what you desire, you will be operating at a lower frequency of manifestation. The mind needs clear images to project when seeking a desired vibrational match. As a result, preferences and details such as "I'd like to find another single parent" are helpful. However, if your highest good takes the form of a single man or woman who is *not* a parent, you will want to be open to that possibility. For instance, you may meet someone who has been in a parental role with his nephew because of his brother's death. He is not technically a parent but certainly is an "acting parent" to this child.

Here is an example of how a person used his imagination to attract a partner:

Frequency Two: Identify Your Desires

Six months ago, Phil broke up with Sally. When he began reflecting on their good times, he decided he wanted a second chance. Sally was now dating others and told Phil she wasn't interested in rekindling their relationship.

Since Phil wanted a relationship, he decided to use the Vibrational Matching technique to attract someone aligned with his preferences. First, he created a Wish List describing all the qualities he sought in a partner—many of which Sally reflected. In addition, he drew up a list of all the gifts he brought to a relationship. This made him feel more confident that he could attract someone new.

Here is Phil's Wish List. Notice how complete it is, and that he has opened himself up to his highest good. Phil now knows that he may bring in someone with even more harmonious qualities than he can imagine.

Phil's Wish List
- Relationship that allows personal freedom for both parties
- Mutually supportive—understanding of my work travel schedule
- She enjoys her work
- She has a life outside of our relationship, e.g., friends, hobbies, work that she loves
- Age range: 34–45
- Enjoys watching sports
- Responsible person
- Financially secure
- Generous and thoughtful with money and time
- Open to marriage
- Highly values our relationship. Both of us create space and time for each other
- Open to bringing children into our lives
- Prosperity-conscious (sees the glass as half full)
- Sincere, genuine, honest

- Positive and optimistic
- Neat and organized
- Playful and lighthearted
- Great friend
- Great lover—sexy, adventurous
- Flexible person
- Likes animals, especially dogs
- Physically fit and health conscious
- At least 5'5" tall, medium weight and body type
- Confident in herself
- Good communicator
- Spiritual beliefs compatible with my own
- Vegetarian
- Supportive of her partner
- Able to bond with me on all levels: physically, emotionally, spiritually, and psychologically
- Support each other's growth in all areas of our lives
- Enhances my life so that I feel higher levels of joy in all aspects of my life
- All of the above or whatever is for my highest good and the highest good for all concerned

Within six months, Phil met Suzanne, who matched all of his desires. She, too, was ready for a loving relationship. They lived together for a year and then married, choosing to postpone having children. "We love our life so much as it is, we just want to focus on each other for a while," Suzanne happily confessed.

IF YOU DESIRE LIFELONG COMMITMENT

If you desire to attract a romantic relationship that will be lifelong, you may want to consider adding the following two items to your Wish List:

1. Able to bond with me on all levels including physically, emotionally, spiritually, and psychologically.
2. As we evolve and change we will fully support each other's growth.

Relationships that are happy and last a lifetime are bonds that are formed on all levels. In addition, as we support each other in our growth, the bond between two people gets even more solidified. Challenges that some relationships cannot withstand will be growth producing and enhancing for others. The difference is in whether or not the bond exists on all levels, and in the commitment for each person to grow.

HIGHEST GOOD FOR ALL CONCERNED

Hold that Wish List! Before you send out your desires, be sure you've attached these five priceless words to the end: "Highest Good for All Concerned." They can make an enormous difference in what you attract.

In fact, when you energetically direct your desires out into the Universe, you might have the best Wish List in the world. When you add, "May this be for the highest good for all concerned," your vibration opens up to attract people, situations, and other gifts aligned with the highest good of the sender and anyone else affected, such as the recipient or children. In fact, something even better than you have asked for may be on its way, since you asked for "your highest good" to be a factor.

Tricia had not been in a relationship for several years and visited a Vibrational Counselor in St. Louis, Missouri, in search of a wonderful partner. She eagerly followed the advice of her counselor and created her Wish List. She included "the highest good for all concerned" at the end of the list, and looked forward to the results.

Six months later, Tricia met Hank, a handsome Navy man who was a friend of her landlord. Although he was on his way back east to his base near Atlanta, he asked if they could write to each other. Tricia enthusiastically agreed. Four months later, he wrote and asked if she would be willing to visit him in Georgia.

Tricia returned with an engagement ring on her hand, put her home up for sale, and moved closer to Hank. "I know I'm doing the right thing. He's the most important person in my life," she told friends, who cautioned her that she did not really know Hank that well.

After three months, Hank stopped calling. He wouldn't even return her e-mails. Tricia called her counselor and asked, "How could this have happened? I asked for a relationship that would be in the highest good for all concerned!"

"Relax, and know that your highest good is coming," advised her counselor. "Focus your attention on other things that are important to you and that give you pleasure. Once you raise your vibratory level, you'll be open to receiving your highest good. This is a time for trust; just know that your desire will be fulfilled. Your life is in perfect order."

Tricia took her counselor's advice to heart. She joined a swim team at her local YMCA, and a month later, as a result of moving to Georgia, she met Barry, the swim instructor and another Missouri native. Gradually, they began to date and their affection blossomed into love. Tricia's faith had opened her up to a vibration equal to her highest good and resulted in her attracting a partner who was *completely* aligned with her desires.

Another example involves Andrea, who was very specific about the details of her intended match. She even had a picture of him! His name was Mark, and he was her fellow trainer at the health club.

Andrea tried Vibrational Matching, but not surprisingly, she did not get the result she desired. She finally visited a Vibrational Counselor to find out what she could do differently to experience a more positive outcome. She learned that by focusing on one specific person, rather than his qualities, she was coming from a place of need or lack, which always translates to a lower vibration. Her happiness and peace of mind were dependent on Mark's interest in her. Since she had not been open to the highest good for all concerned, she kept her desires just outside her reach, and could not possibly be a vibrational match to what she wanted.

Andrea decided to try again, and with her counselor's help, created a new Wish List. This time, she listed the qualities she admired in Mark and added others that she desired. She also included Mark on her Wish List, but added, "If this is for my highest good and the highest good for all concerned."

Mark never expressed an interest in Andrea; however, within one month, Andrea met Al, who had just been hired to coach her daughter's soccer team.

Al's love of athletics and his cheerful personality were an instant hit with Andrea, and five years later, they are married with two more children. By choosing to focus on the highest good for all concerned, rather than on a specific individual, Andrea came from a place of strength. This significantly raised her vibration and her attraction power, enabling her to manifest Al, who matched her desire for a partner for herself and a father for her daughter.

The ability to attract the relationship you desire hinges on your ability to be clear about what you want. A Wish List is one way to achieve clarity. By writing down your needs and desires, you can recognize more easily what you want to manifest.

Pass the Lemonade, Please

Joan and Bill are at it again! "You never pick up after yourself," she chastises him. "I can't live in this chaos!"

"Well I can't live with a complainer," Bill retorts, trying to relax after a hard day at work. "All you ever do is gripe and complain. What's happened to you, anyway?"

When you have an experience that isn't working for you, it is easy to become angry and defensive. The trouble is, it does not get you anywhere except even angrier, thus lowering your vibratory level.

Instead, you can actually transcend this kind of situation by recognizing it as an opportunity to create a better one. Here's how Joan can make "lemonade out of lemons" with Bill.

First, Joan can stop the cycle of blame. Rather than trying to change Bill, Joan can ask herself, "What new desire has evolved from this situation?"

Now Joan can shift into a more positive mode. By focusing on her desired outcome, rather than on what's not working, she can begin to energize what she wishes.

"I want to live in a neat, clean space," she said thoughtfully. "Maybe we can hire a maid. My preference is that things work out with Bill, if this is in our highest good."

As Joan became more optimistic, she began to raise her vibration to a level where she had access to potential solutions. Solutions to challenging situations arrive when we turn our thoughts toward our desires rather than focusing attention on what we do not want.

As Joan tuned in to various options, she shifted her energies from feeling helpless and angry to feeling a ray of hope. Within two weeks, something amazing happened. Bill began occasionally picking up after himself, and then on a fairly regular basis. Joan, grateful that she and Bill were feeling better about each other, began bringing home surprise tokens of appreciation for him. Bill was especially delighted the night she brought home tickets for the Ravens game.

What happened? It is a universal truth that when one partner lets go of a negative thought pattern directed at the other partner, both raise their vibrations. Joan trusted that her desire would be met in one form or another, and relaxed her grip on Bill's messiness. Bill became more open to accepting Joan's desire for organization. Once he began cooperating with her, he had fun with his newly reformed status, teasing Joan that everything was really hidden in their coat closet.

Joan actually learned an important lesson from this experience. "I discovered that getting angry only attracts more reasons to be upset. And it certainly doesn't change anyone's behavior. When I let go and focused on my desired outcome, Bill became more open and willing to work with me."

Bill's higher vibration and desire to have a harmonious relationship with Joan inspired him to take action; however, resolution can take many forms, such as hiring a housekeeper. It is important to remember that when you raise your vibration, you have access to thoughts that are aligned with solutions. On the other hand, when you struggle, resist, or fight against something, you energetically stay entangled with the things you do not want and attract more of the same.

THE POWER OF POSITIVE IMAGERY

Once you have identified the characteristics of the type of person you want to attract, you can energize the relationship through visualization. Imagery brings greater clarity, and it increases positive emotion, preparing you to move on to Frequency Three—Activate Your Intentions. Guidelines for creating successful imagery include:

1. Always imagine success in attracting the person of your dreams.

2. See the relationship as though it already exists. Imagine doing your favorite things with this person and sharing intimate moments.

Tune into Love

3. Focus on the end result, e.g., if you desire marriage then
   see yourself married. Visualize the wedding band on
   your hand and living in your ideal house. Be as detailed
   as possible while maintaining positive emotion.
4. Allow yourself to enjoy the emotions associated with
   being with your perfect partner. Visualize being happy,
   laughing and fulfilled in your day-to-day life.

Do I know what I want?
Did I create this relationship?

How could it be so?

Never would we meet on an internet site
We have nothing in common, but it seemed so right

The stars in the heavens lined up above
And a perfect stranger introduced us
Is it love?

It seemed so easy, at least to my friends
That I should go out so seldom
And meet a man

Little did they know the work I had done
Envisioning this guy and my house in the sun

Many nights I sat home with my beach pictures around
Seeing my dream of this wonderful guy and my beach house in
the sand

My thoughts must have been too shallow you see
I ended up with a wonderful guy with a beautiful beach house
But did he love me?

Back to the drawing board to envision the emotional bond
Fine tuning my vibration so I'm able to move on

—Mona McLaughlin

FREQUENCY TWO: LOVE BOOSTERS

Identify Your Desires

- Create a lighthearted mood, light some candles, play some soothing music, and write a Wish List identifying the qualities of your ideal relationship. Create a sacred space for your desires. Consider wrapping a box with your favorite wrapping paper and place your Wish List in there along with other symbols of love, such as a heart-shaped candle, rose petals, a feather, or your favorite charm.

- Create a mandala representing your desirable new relationship. Use crayons, markers, computer graphics, or anything else that suits your fancy. Follow Carl Jung's example and construct a new one each day, if you like, and hang them on your bedroom wall.

- Meditate daily using whatever technique feels comfortable for you. If you have created a mandala, consider using it as a tool in meditation, or use the one provided for you in this book (chapter 3).

- Every day, create some "feel-good" moments by thinking about your new relationship. When you are in a peaceful, harmonious state of mind, imagine what it would be like to be with this wonderful person. Imagine the two of you laughing and enjoying your companionship. See yourselves dining at your favorite restaurant or by candlelight at your home. See yourselves watching a romantic comedy and laughing nonstop.

- Now take a hot bath, light some incense, play some music, and savor the scenes you have created.

FREQUENCY TWO AT-A-GLANCE REFERENCE GUIDE

- Lighten up! Be playful. Be grateful. Have fun with this process in co-creation.

Tune into Love

- While in a state of gratitude, play some inspiring, uplifting music, and create a written Wish List of preferences you have for your ideal partner. Aim high and use your imagination to the fullest as you create with enthusiasm. Regardless of your present circumstances see yourself as whole, happy, emotionally and physically healthy. Approach this exercise from a place of optimism while recognizing the abundance of the Universe.

- If you are having difficulty identifying your preferences, then take a moment and jot down undesirable characteristics of individuals you've attracted in the past or present. Across from each undesirable characteristic list the opposite. Include on your Wish List whatever seems appealing to you. For example, an undesirable quality might be argumentative. The opposite could be defined as communicates clearly, harmoniously, and respectfully. As you do this part of the exercise be sure and focus attention on what you desire. Pause and give attention to what is undesirable for only a very brief moment, and as a mechanism to gain clarity of your desire if you feel it would be helpful.

- If this agrees with you, include on your Wish List: someone I can bond with on all possible levels, e.g., emotionally, physically, intellectually, and spiritually. Also include, "my highest good and the highest good for all concerned."

- Each day pay close attention to the characteristics of others and make additions to your Wish List as you see qualities that appeal to you. Your list is a *work in progress,* so feel free to change it as often as you like. Clarity comes from reflecting on and acknowledging the things we attract whether we like or dislike what we are allowing in our lives.

- Keep your list private. This is between you and your source energy.

- Take time each day to close your eyes and quiet your mind. Listen rather than talk. Relax, rather than think. Just breathe deeply and allow thoughts and images from source energy to be impressed on your mind. Fully allow yourself to bathe in this unconditional love as you absorb warmth, light, images, and messages.

Chapter Seven
Frequency Three: Activate Your Intentions

When I look into the future, it's so bright, it burns my eyes.

—Oprah Winfrey

Congratulations! You have now moved through the first two frequencies—Create "Feel-Good" Moments and Identify Your Desires. You are now beginning to feel the high vibration that comes with a positive focus. You are also able to identify exactly what you wish to create.

It is time to add Frequency Three to your vibration. This stage can be compared to lighting the fuel inside the booster rocket that will speed your "intention" towards its desired vibrational match.

What do we mean by "intention"? Although there are many dictionary definitions, when we refer to the process of Vibrational Matching, intention has a special definition: the blending of strong desire and strong belief.

Both desire and belief provide the "emotional fuel" to

launch our mental booster rocket with power and precision. The level of desire for something, and the strength of belief that you can attract it, strongly influence how quickly the matching desire will be brought to you.

DESIRE AND BELIEF: FUEL FOR THE JOURNEY

Jerry had a very strong desire for a relationship. When he learned about Vibrational Matching, his enthusiasm was high, and he created his Wish List like a pro. He sailed through all the steps, enjoyed the Love Boosters, and was ready to transmit his strong desire and intention for a relationship that would be in his highest good and the highest good for all concerned.

Then, just before he was ready to begin, he told his older brother, Tom, what he was about to do. "You've got to be kidding," Tom scoffed. "Do you really believe in that stuff?"

At that moment, a seed of doubt was planted in Jerry's mind, and his belief in his ability to attract a relationship began to waver. Recognizing what was happening, he asked Les, his Vibrational Counselor, how he could restore his former belief in his ability to manifest a wonderful partner.

"No problem," Les reassured him. "Just set a new intention. For example, 'I intend to increase my belief that I *can* manifest my desire.' You can also set the intention to be open to receiving every level of support that will strengthen your belief in yourself and your manifestation abilities."

Tom felt far more capable after his session with Les. A few days later, after fortifying himself with positive thoughts and rebuilding his confidence, he proceeded with his first Vibrational Matching opportunity. To his astonishment, Sheila, his next-door neighbor, turned out to be the match he was looking for!

Did you ever find that your feelings guided you in an unexpected direction? For example, you might think that you want to date someone who is attractive, available, and flirtatious with you. However, despite the flattering attention you've received, you have a "gut feeling" that responding to this person would not be in your best interest.

The following is an example of how this would work in relation to Vibrational Matching.

Louise was attracted to Mitchell, her coworker, and was thinking he would be a lot of fun to go out with on a date. Then she had the thought, "Don't do it." This came in the form of a visceral, almost physical manifestation, as well as a "knowing." At first she pushed it aside because logically it didn't make sense. But over and over again, the feeling of unease reasserted itself.

Louise decided to follow her "gut" and ignore Mitchell's flirtatious behavior. She later learned that Mitchell was married, even though he told her he was single. Louise, who desired a monogamous relationship with a man of the highest degree of integrity, later understood why her gut feeling about Mitchell was "right on." She was very glad she had listened to her inner knowing, even though it had no logical base. In this case, the feeling was an early warning that going out on a date with Mitchell was not in alignment with her desire to be in a monogamous relationship with an honest man.

Your feelings stem from your thoughts and lend the attracting power or "fuel" that can move you more quickly towards your desire. If you focus your thoughts on your desire and believe that you will attract it, you will boost your manifestation power considerably. However, this also works in negative situations. If you continue to feed fears that your partner will leave you, he or she may, in time, do just that.

Thoughts that have more emotion attached to them, coupled with a strong belief in them, create a very powerful force for drawing things into your experience. If you are drawing something you desire into your experience, you will feel wonderful. If you are drawing something into your experience that is not aligned with your desires, you will have negative emotion. Pay attention to your feelings—they will give you feedback regarding whether or not you are attracting and creating experiences aligned with your deepest desires.

Our feelings about ourselves are the foundation for the experiences we attract. Whatever we believe about ourselves is confirmed over and over again, since what we give attention to comes into our experience.

- We cannot attract "thin" if we feel "heavy." Instead we will attract more reasons to feel "heavy."
- We cannot attract love if we feel unloved. Instead we will attract more reasons to feel unlovable.
- We cannot attract a date who will appreciate us if we feel unworthy. Instead, we will attract people into our experience who will reinforce our feeling of being unworthy.

Therefore, in order to shift towards our goals and desires, we must feed ourselves a new diet of "self-talk" that reassures us we are worthy, attractive, capable, and lovable. Once we have raised our "self-love" vibration, we can move more confidently towards our desirable vibrational match. The way to do this is to set an intention to feel good about ourselves in every way, including the gifts we can bring to a relationship.

What do we do when a negative thought hangs on, despite our best attempts to let it go? In that case, we can send out a signal to the Universe that we wish to release a fear or concern and have it replaced with loving thoughts that are in our highest good.

Stuart, for example, was eager for a partner, but feared that an intimate relationship might jeopardize his relationship with Ginny, his teenage daughter, who was jealous of other women in his life. Even though he recognized this, he tended to push his concern aside, telling himself, "Things will take care of themselves. I deserve to be happy, and Ginny will just have to accept my new partner."

However, try as he might, Stuart did not use his Vibrational Matching abilities successfully. When his counselor helped him recognize that his fears of distancing his daughter were sabotaging his efforts to find a new partner, he repeated to himself, "This is a belief I held before I understood that I can create my own experiences."

Stuart now had an opportunity to create a new reality, one in which he, his daughter, and his new partner would interact harmoniously. Our ideas about what "reality" is can bind us to the present. Yet, there is a huge gap between the reality we believe we are living, and "true" reality. In fact, the "true" reality is that we are capable of creating whatever experiences we desire, once we identify them, give power to them, and become a vibrational match for them.

For those who have not learned this approach to manifestation, reality is whatever happens to them. For those who have learned Vibrational Matching, reality is whatever they wish it to be. Sound amazing? It is. Once you begin practicing this technique, you will be able to adapt it to every circumstance in life—health, job, social situations, money, or love.

GUIDELINES FOR WRITING INTENTIONS/AFFIRMATIONS

1. Present tense (example: "I have a loving partner" rather than "I'll have a loving partner").

2. Positively focused—give attention to what you desire rather than the lack of it (example: "I have a generous partner" rather than "My partner is not stingy").

3. Personally connected—always about yourself rather than other people; refrain from comparing yourself to others.

4. Words that generate emotion (example: "I am *ecstatic* about the romantic vacation I'm going on with my partner").

5. Believable—the stronger your belief the more powerful is your attraction.

6. Ideal oriented—focus on achieving your goal (example: "Our wedding plans are going smoothly. . . . everything is perfect").

7. Results oriented—focus on the end result rather than the process (example: "I met a really nice guy" rather than "I met a really nice guy *by playing tennis*").

8. Highest degree of integrity—focus on what *your* heart desires rather than what *others* want for you or what you *think* you "should" want (example: "He must be college educated because that will make my family happy").

9. Routinely set intentions for higher levels of joy in all areas of your life.

SAMPLE LIST OF INTENTIONS/AFFIRMATIONS

1. I am optimistic about all aspects of my life. I trust in my ability to attract and create my highest good.

2. I always attract relationships and circumstances that are in my highest good.

3. All my relationships are in perfect order and aligned with my destiny.

4. I am grateful for all the relationships and life circumstances that have prepared me to attract and allow the perfect partner for me.

5. I have attracted the relationship of my dreams. This relationship is in my highest good. I lovingly receive this gift from the Universe.

6. My partner has the highest degree of integrity.

7. My partner and I are compatible in every way. We have created an emotional, physical, spiritual, and intellectual bond.

8. I am now experiencing absolute joy and prosperity in all aspects of my life.

9. I am grateful for the loving partner that I have attracted into my life.

10. My partner and I are traveling together through Europe. This trip is synchronized perfectly to attract great joy.

Dream Capture

Discover your dream
Imagine it
Wish upon a star
Believe in its reality come true
Affirm the works in progress
Thank the Universe
                    —Mary McCraw-Borst © 1997

FREQUENCY THREE: LOVE BOOSTERS

Activate Your Intentions

- Think of a mentor or role model who has successfully attracted a desirable romantic relationship. Ask that person to quietly "hold the vision" of your desirable partner coming to fruition.

- Create a list of all the attributes you bring to a relationship. Include aspects of your personality such as: sense of humor, loving, thoughtful, open-minded, insightful, well-rounded, generous, emotionally secure, etc.

- Write positive intentions to support you in attracting your desirable relationship.

- Every day spend 5–10 minutes combining positive imagery with your intentions for this relationship. Choose a time when you are relaxed and in a peaceful state of mind. Create sacred space around this relationship by lighting some candles, listening to music, or being in nature.

Frequency Three at-a-Glance Reference Guide

- Lighten up! Be playful. Be grateful. Have fun with this process in co-creation.

- Correlate your thoughts, beliefs, and feelings with what you are attracting into your experience. Reflect on this daily. Low vibrations of anger, hate, shame, guilt, despair, being offended or victimized are all indicators of judgment toward self or others that reflects insecurity or lack of self-love. Judgment toward self or others creates vibrational disharmony, and delays as well as prohibits our desires from coming to fruition.

- Tune in to your feelings. When you feel *upbeat* your thoughts and beliefs *are* aligned with your intentions/desires. That *upbeat* feeling is a high frequency level. When you feel *down* this lower frequency level is telling you that your thoughts and beliefs are *not* in alignment with your intentions/desires.

- Set the intention to believe in your ability to manifest all you desire. The Universe will take care of bringing whatever you need to increase your self-confidence. Be open and pay attention to the synchronistic events that will occur as a result of this intention. Belief is enhanced by releasing the limitations of your past, historical data or trends, and realistic thinking. Instead, focus on possibilities and opportunities.

- Have fun thinking about being with your ideal mate. Allow yourself to feel the excitement and passion for this new relationship without putting your happiness or piece of mind on hold waiting for your dreams to come to fruition. When we are in a "waiting mode" our vibration lowers because energetically we are focused on what we feel is lacking. Go on and live your life to the fullest each day.

- Practice visualization while in a lighthearted and enthusiastic state of mind. Use the following techniques:
  - See yourself as whole and happy.
  - Think of yourself as being a couple with this person.

Frequency Three: Activate Your Intentions

- Imagine success and see the relationship in the present.
- Stay focused on the desirable outcome rather than the process of getting there.
- Be action-oriented. See yourself having wonderful interactions with your partner, e.g., watching a funny movie and laughing together, or enjoying other common interests, etc.
- Let yourself feel enthused about this person and the new relationship.
- Create imagery in your mind that is believable on some level to you. Stretching to believe is a good sign that you are being optimistic rather than realistic. Optimism is very helpful in this process.
- Keep your visualization private, or share thoughtfully with someone who can mentor and encourage you in the process of Vibrational Matching. You only need your energy coupled with the Universe to create this relationship.
- Be a visionary and stay focused on the desired outcome rather than the reality of your present circumstances. Reality roots us to our present situation whereas imagination brings us closer to our dreams.
- Be open and focus on the abundance of the Universe. Scarcity mindset will only attract more of the same. Walk with confidence in the direction of your dreams and you will be provided for along the way.
- Don't worry about *how* you will attract this person. Just know that he/she is coming. Leave the process up to the higher, quicker vibration of the Universe.
- Maintain integrity by being true to your desires rather than deny they exist. Stay personally connected to your ideal image of a relationship. Refrain from comparing yourself to others or giving attention to what others want for you.
- Allow your actions to be inspired. Often those "out of the blue" ideas are moments of inspiration from a higher energy source. Spontaneity may be an indicator of being tuned in to source energy.
- Take time each day to close your eyes and quiet your

Tune into Love

mind. Listen rather than talk. Relax rather than think. Just breathe deeply and allow thoughts and images from source energy to be impressed on your mind. Fully allow yourself to bathe in this unconditional love as you absorb warmth, light, images, and messages.

Chapter Eight
Frequency Four: Release the Outcome

There's nothing left to say
There's nothing else to do
But close my eyes, look inside
And to myself be true

—Jon Riggle

Releasing the outcome means that you trust in a power beyond your conscious mind to bring you the right partner. Since the discovery of quantum physics, it has been agreed that vibrations do in fact exist, and that they attract frequencies of the same level. Since we cannot see them, we often doubt that these unseen energies can work for us. In fact, the Law of Attraction can be very effective in helping us transcend fears and other deterrents to success. When we raise our vibrations, set intentions, and *release the outcome for our highest good*, our wishes can be reflected back to us with unerring accuracy.

Seymour is an accountant who created a detailed Wish

List, went through all the preliminary stages of Vibrational Matching with flying colors, and sent out his desire for a woman who would be financially secure and responsible with money, among other desirable qualities. His Wish List ended with, "This, or whatever is for the highest good for all concerned." Then, he consciously released the outcome and waited for his desirable vibrational match to arrive.

Six months later, he met Claudia. She was everything he wanted except for one quality: she had just gone through a bankruptcy.

Seymour knew that Claudia was a one-in-a-million match for him. They were compatible in every way. Despite his friends' concerns ("She's irresponsible when it comes to money. Look at her track record."), Seymour had a strong "sense" that Claudia was the woman for him.

This feeling was *not* based on logic, nor was it based on "blind" feelings of being in love. It was simply a strong "knowing" that staying in the relationship and allowing himself time to get to know her would be in his highest good. He did not want to be hasty and leave the relationship, nor did he think a marriage proposal was in order. He trusted himself to make the "right" decision in time, and that the outcome would be perfect.

Seymour was glad he listened to his intuition. Six months after they met, Claudia landed a top-notch position with a major record company and brought in a much higher salary than he did. Needless to say, the partnership has flourished and Claudia and Seymour now own two homes in California and a cottage in New England, most of which is financed by Claudia.

In fact, because Claudia had learned from her earlier experiences, she was an even more responsible and capable partner than one who had not experienced financial trouble. If Seymour had judged Claudia by her apparent "reality" when they met, he might have closed down and looked for another partner. But his "gut," or intuition, clearly indicated that Claudia was capable of creating her own financial security without relying on him.

When we release the outcome we feel peaceful inside. This makes it possible to tune into our intuition and receive higher guidance. When we allow guidance from a higher perspective to flow through us, we experience a strong sense of knowing without it necessarily being reality based. Over time, as we have experience in allowing our intuition to guide us in creating our dreams and in decision-making, we trust that everything will work out for our highest good.

Releasing the outcome implies that you have confidence in your ability to succeed. By focusing on the desired outcome, seeing yourself happily partnered with the right person, and experiencing feelings of joy and contentment, you will raise your vibration to attract your desires.

As you become aware of fears that can impede your ability to bring in the partner you desire, replace them with the intention to be open to lovingly receiving your new partner. Stay focused on the feelings of contentment and fulfillment that await you, and know that you will attract the vibrational match you desire.

Remember the Law of Allowing and what we resist persists. This applies to what we defend against, worry about, prepare for, and the things with which we struggle. You will note that all of the above are based on fear, which is a very low vibration. Until we replace resistance with love, we will continue to attract similar experiences and live our self-fulfilling prophecies.

Donna was nervous about the Fourth Frequency. Her friends called her a "control freak," and she had driven away several potential partners by her demands. When she came to seek help from Laurie, her Los Angeles Vibrational Counselor, she loved the idea of controlling her life through her thoughts but was uneasy about the "letting go" part of the Vibrational Matching process.

When Laurie pointed out that her controlling nature was

fueled by her fears, Donna agreed to work through some of them with her. They finally came to the point of releasing them, and Donna was ready to accept whatever her "highest good" would bring her.

It was no surprise to find that Jim, her vibrational match, was a man who had also dealt with a need to control others and was now sensitive to letting people run their own lives. Between them, Donna and Jim have shifted their thinking to focus on controlling what they bring into their own lives, rather than trying to take responsibility for the lives of others (a highly stressful, as well as impossible, task). For Donna and Jim, life is now a series of wonderful adventures.

Releasing the outcome of the Vibrational Matching process is an enlightening journey. In order to be truly successful at releasing, we must come from a place of strength; controlling behavior stems from insecurities based on fear. Releasing enables us to be in control of our experiences because we have the knowledge and skill to create our own reality.

As we perfect our skills in Vibrational Matching we understand that life is a series of desires that, when met, stimulate new desires. See exhibit G to further your understanding of this point.

As we learn to release the outcome, and set intentions for our highest good, as discussed in chapter 6, the result may be different than what we had hoped for. However, in time, we unfold into a new understanding and are grateful that we did not get our wish. I can demonstrate this using my friend Linda as an example. Linda, who was dating Jay, had been clear all along that she wanted her highest good, so when Jay proposed she jumped to the conclusion that this was meant to be, and said yes, against her better judgment. One day, quite unexpectedly, Jay canceled the engagement a few months before the wedding. At first Linda was devastated, but later she confessed to me that she knew in her heart that this was not the best relationship for her. Now, happily married to

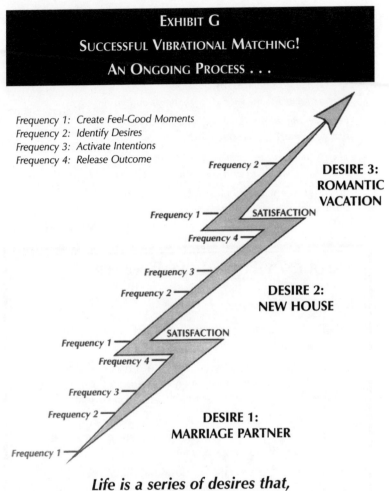

EXHIBIT G

SUCCESSFUL VIBRATIONAL MATCHING!

AN ONGOING PROCESS . . .

Frequency 1: Create Feel-Good Moments
Frequency 2: Identify Desires
Frequency 3: Activate Intentions
Frequency 4: Release Outcome

Frequency 2 —

DESIRE 3:
ROMANTIC
VACATION

Frequency 1 — SATISFACTION

Frequency 4 —

Frequency 3 —

Frequency 2 —

DESIRE 2:
NEW HOUSE

SATISFACTION

Frequency 1 —

Frequency 4 —

Frequency 3 —

Frequency 2 —

DESIRE 1:
MARRIAGE PARTNER

Frequency 1 —

Life is a series of desires that,
when met,
stimulate new desires.

Kevin, with two delightful children, Linda is very grateful to the Universe that her wedding plans with Jay were canceled.

Releasing your wish to attract your highest good is the most positive action you can take. Go on, take the plunge; the water is incredibly inviting. You will discover that once you do, your life can flow with effortless ease and you can travel from one great adventure to another.

Tune into Love

There are many available partners that are perfect for me
and my energy is exactly where it needs to be

I attract from my vibration that is here and now
I am so excited because I understand how

The choice is mine, it is my decision
I create what I want with clear thoughts and vision

I believe and allow—knowing without any doubt
that my thoughts do create what I send out

The frequency of my perfect other tunes in
and that "chance" meeting happens and it's time to begin

If it's not to my liking I must take a look at myself
shifting what's necessary to attract something else

—Mona McLaughlin

FREQUENCY FOUR: LOVE BOOSTERS

Release the Outcome

- Regularly practice a mind-body technique, such as yoga, tai chi, qi gong, etc.

- Align your energy by utilizing the services of a certified massage therapist, licensed acupuncturist, reiki, healing touch, or other healthcare professional.

- Make a list of *fun* things to do *without* a partner. Focus your attention on things that are rewarding to you. Do these things regularly.

- Create a "success list" of desirable things, people, or situations that you have previously manifested, such as a great friendship, new job, scholarship, etc. Remember how you felt when your desire came to fruition and savor the memory.

- Write your own fantasy love story with a very happy ending. Be sure to include a lot of juicy moments.

- Imagine sending your desires out into the Universe via a special messenger bird who will carry your invitation to the perfect person for you. A special meeting is being arranged for the two of you in the very near future—at the perfect time and place.

FREQUENCY FOUR AT-A-GLANCE REFERENCE GUIDE

- Lighten up! Be playful. Be grateful. Have fun with this process in co-creation.

- Live in the present. Get on with your life *knowing* your desires will show up at the perfect time and in the perfect way. If you try to rush things you will keep your desires just beyond your reach. You cannot force the rose to bloom. It will bloom when the time is ready. For now, enjoy watching the rose unfold gloriously.

- Release fear by setting the intention to trust in your ability to manifest your highest good. As you attune to synchronistic events in your life you will come to realize how connected you are to a pool of Universal intelligence that will guide you step by step. Continually set intentions that will support you in feeling confident in bringing forth the ideal partner.

- Put good thoughts around all your desires, yet get on with your life. Look forward with pleasure to what you are creating. Open yourself to love. Let your dreams unfold naturally. Worrying or trying to rush things simply lowers your vibration and slows down the process. Just let things unfold naturally and allow yourself to be inspired into action.

- Reframe undesirable situations to see them from a higher and more optimistic perspective. Barriers in your relationship with other people and with yourself are created because of beliefs and assumptions. These are within your control and can be changed. Be guided by the Law of Allowing, which is freedom from negativity. As you release judgment of what you or others are attracting you release negative emotion. Allowing is different from tolerating. Tolerating is feeling like you have to "put up" with something or someone. The key to following the law of Allowing is believing that your highest good is in the outcome of every situation.

- Take time daily for quiet reflection and communing with nature. Even ten minutes a day can bring about huge results in keeping your vibration high.

Tune into Love

- Always remember when one door closes another door opens. When you open to your highest good, doors will shut to guide you to a better place. As you allow these doors to shut lovingly, you open yourself up to new doors opening, which will reflect your highest good. Your ideal relationship is on its way. Stay focused on what is coming and have fun daydreaming about him/her while you get involved with other interesting activities.

- Relax and open to all of your emotions rather than struggle or deny feelings that are uncomfortable. Set the intention to unify and bring harmony to your mind, body, and spirit. This will create the energy force to enable you to find resolution and allow you to receive your highest good.

- Take time each day to quiet your mind as you meditate. Listen rather than talk. Relax rather than think. Just breathe deeply and allow thoughts and images from source energy to be impressed on your mind. Fully allow yourself to bathe in this unconditional love as you absorb warmth, light, images, and messages.

Part Three

Frequently Asked Questions

What If You Tuned into Love?

*What if fairies really do exist
throughout the Universe, in the mist,
to help us create our heavenly bliss?*

*And what if you were willing to do
whatever they asked of you?*

*And in the next hour,
you would have your power.*

*What would you do
to bring in the new?*

*Would you look in the mirror and say,
I love you with all my heart and soul,
each and every day?
Oh, you wonderful being of light,
I will be true to you each and every night.*

Tune into Love

Would you speak these words loud and clear
so your prince or princess could appear?

Would you release the night
to allow the light?

It is up to you
to allow your dreams to come true.
My dear, dear friend,
what will you do?

—Margaret McCraw, November 26, 2004

Frequently Asked Questions about Attracting a Relationship

Let it be easy. Struggle is not required.
—Alan Cohen

How is Vibrational Matching different from positive thinking? I have been thinking positively about attracting a mate for a year and I am still waiting for him to appear.
—Positively Pooped Out, Los Angeles, California

Vibrational Matching takes the concept of positive thinking to a feeling level. Each of us offers a distinct vibration for every desire we have. Our dominant vibration is what attracts our experiences, and is determined by the combined frequency of our thoughts, beliefs, and feelings regarding a particular desire.

We may be offering positive thoughts by saying, "I am looking forward to meeting a great guy and I know someone is out there for me," but deep down, we're really feeling, "I am tired of waiting and I really doubt that I will meet someone. All the research shows it is practically impossible to get married after 'a certain age.'"

Positive thinking is the first step to attracting our desires; however, believing in ourselves and our ability to create what we want results in positive feelings. The emotion attached to a particular desire, positive or negative, has great influence in creating a dominant frequency that either attracts or repels our dreams.

How long will it take me to find my desirable vibrational match?

—Anxiously Waiting, Austin, Texas

Your desirable vibrational match is just around the corner. He or she will show up when you are truly "ready" to receive him or her into your life.

When you are in a "waiting" mode, you are placing your happiness or peace of mind "on hold" by giving attention to what you do not have. This keeps it just beyond your reach. The more attention you give to what you do not have, the more pessimistic your thoughts become, which lowers your vibration. You may meet potential dates but none of them may be desirable by your standards.

You will be a vibrational match to your desires when you take yourself "off hold" and truly believe that the right person for you will arrive in perfect timing. Get happy without a partner. Feel peaceful without a partner, and know that he or she is on the way.

What happens if I use these techniques and the man I attract isn't what I want?

—High Expectations, San Francisco, California

Then it is time to make a new "Wish List," clarifying what

you want, and turning your attention toward your new desire. For instance, if he has cats and you're allergic to them, write in your "Wish List": My ideal mate's living situation is compatible with me in every way. Remember to ask for "your highest good and the highest good for all concerned."

What's the difference between a desirable vibrational match and just any vibrational match?

—Inquisitive, Honolulu, Hawaii

We are always a vibrational match to what we are currently attracting. This means we are giving attention through our thoughts (consciously or unconsciously) to what we desire or what we fear.

Vibrational Matching is the process of purposefully raising our vibration in order to attract what we desire such as an ideal mate rather than just a mate. It is the deliberate intention to energize what we want by aligning and unifying our thoughts, beliefs, and emotions in the direction of our desires.

I am sick and tired of meeting women who expect me to pay for every date. I would like to meet someone who shares in this responsibility. How can I turn what I am currently attracting into something desirable using Vibrational Matching techniques?

—Deal Breaker, Marco Island, Florida

What we resist persists! To attract something different, you must become a vibrational match to what you desire rather than what you dislike.

In this situation, writing on your "Wish List" that you want to meet women who split the tab is a good "positive thinking" first step. Now, let's take it beyond positive thinking and actually raise your vibration by shifting your feelings about this issue.

For example, you might shift your feelings by saying, "There are no clear rules about dating and everyone is different. Many women have been with men who expect and actually like to pay the bill. It's hard for men and women to know what to expect when dating someone new. A friendly conversation about this with my date could clear the air and keep communication open. Perhaps my date would even be relieved to talk about this."

The goal here is to access thoughts that bring you to a higher vibration which you will recognize as a "better feeling tone" about this issue. Once you've been successful in doing this you will be a vibrational match for your desire rather than what you are resisting.

I created a Wish List and included "for my highest good and the highest good for all concerned." I met a great woman whom I like very much, but there are a few qualities she lacks that I would like in a long-term companion. Should I forget about trying to attract someone else and assume she is in my best interest?
—Highest Good Pending, Reno, Nevada

It may be in your highest good to be with this individual; however, that does not necessarily translate into her being your long-term mate. Sometimes we attract individuals into our experience as preparation for a committed partnership or to help us identify deeper desires. These individuals are still in our highest good even though we may not be in a relationship with them forever.

Consider revising your Wish List to incorporate your new preferences. If your current partner is a vibrational match for your desires, then it will become obvious in time. Pay attention to your feelings when you are with her, and let happiness be your guiding light.

Frequently Asked Questions

Why is it that men always leave me?

—Lady in Waiting, Peach Tree City, Georgia

Your question implies that you feel rejected, and that you are questioning your own self-worth. Allow the men in your life to make choices, without judging them and without judging yourself. As you become an allower, your feelings toward yourself will be more positive, strengthening your attraction power for your desires.

When our partners leave they are not rejecting us; they are simply saying yes to something else in their life. If someone is not ready to receive the love you can offer, then they will not stay.

To raise your vibration, consciously stop focusing attention on men leaving and visualize them staying. As you begin to believe in the possibility of having your desires, your dominant vibration will shift to support you in creating all that you want.

My sister and I both made our "Wish Lists" and put good thoughts around our desires. She met a great guy—I'm still waiting for a date. Why? What went wrong?

—Ticked Off, Salina, Kansas

As long as you are in a waiting mode you will continue to be at a standstill. Shift your focus from waiting, longing, and wanting someone to make you happy, to having fun. As you let go of trying so hard, and enjoy being with yourself, you will attract your desires.

I made my Wish List and prioritized it. I forgot to add "neat and organized" because it did not seem important. Now, a great guy has appeared but he is really disorganized and messy. It is driving me nuts. What do I do now?

—Forgetful Suzy, Washington, D.C.

Add "neat and organized" to your Wish List and have fun seeing how the situation plays out. Stay focused on your preferences rather than on his messiness. Perhaps he will be inspired to hire someone to do housekeeping chores. If it is in your highest good for the two of you to be together, the situation will resolve itself lovingly, and in time.

I am 82 years old. Am I too "old" to use Vibrational Matching techniques? Do you think there is an ideal woman out there who could be attracted to me?

—Hopeful, Seattle, Washington

Abundance does not have age limits. The Universe is limitless in its ability to provide us with our desires. As you open your mind and believe in abundance, you will have access to your desires. If you focus on scarcity you will attract more reasons to experience lack in your life.

My fiancé and I get along fantastically, but his son and I have a lot of conflict. What can I do to hang on to my guy without going nuts?

—Going Crazy, Reading, Pennsylvania

First of all, be aware of your language. When you are "hanging on" to something you are not coming from a place of strength; thus you cannot be a vibrational match for your desires. Shift your focus to the quality of your relationship rather than holding on to your partner.

Set intentions to create a loving harmonious relationship with the son, one that is in the highest good for all concerned. Allow yourself to be inspired to create something different from what the past might dictate. Stay open and allow yourself to be guided by your intuition. Let your actions be inspired.

I don't think I am attractive by traditional standards, but I do everything I can to look good. I would like to attract a great-looking guy. Do I have a chance?

—Good-Looking, St. Augustine, Florida

Your ability to attract your desires is highly influenced by how you feel about yourself. If you value yourself and what you bring to a relationship, you will attract someone who is appealing to you.

Can I just think about my Wish List or must I write it down? I don't want anyone else to see it and I live with a bunch of "nosey" people.

—Privacy Wanted, Houston, Texas

Your list does not need to be in writing. However, a written list helps us to clarify our thoughts. It also helps us to track and correlate our preferences with what we are actually attracting into our life.

My astrologer tells me I'm in a seven-month "drought cycle" with men. Should I wait until it's over to try and attract my desirable match?

—Delayed by the Stars, Albuquerque, New Mexico

Our personal vibration can transcend astrological cycles, if you believe it can. Why wait when you can fulfill your desires now?

I have health concerns. Is there hope for me to attract a desirable vibrational match?

—Hopeful, Salem, Massachusetts

There is an abundance of potential desirable matches for you. When we feel optimistic our attraction power is strong. Stay with the high vibration of feeling hopeful and you will experience firsthand the limitlessness of the Universe to provide your desires.

I would like to attract a woman who does not mind living in the country. I love being in nature, but most women I meet like being in the city. Is there any chance that I can meet a kindred "woodsy spirit" using Vibrational Matching techniques?

—Nesting in the Woods, Richfield, Utah

Write it on your Wish List and visualize her nestled in the woods with you. Our imagination helps us create the "feeling tone" of our desires. Be playful with your fantasies and as you begin to experience her in your mind she will become part of your real-life experience.

What factor does timing play in meeting your desirable vibrational match?

—Tic Toc, Santa Monica, California

The stronger and more positive your dominant vibration is about a particular desire, the more quickly you will become a vibrational match to it. When you are open to your highest good, the timing will be coordinated perfectly with all of your desires.

All of the guys I attract end up being "emotionally unavailable." This is certainly opposite of what I desire. How can I change this?

—Vibrating Heart, Chicago, Illinois

You are holding "emotionally unavailable" in your vibration for one of two reasons:
   a. You are emotionally unavailable and/or
   b. You are focusing your thoughts on others being emotionally unavailable.

Tune into Love

There are many available partners that are perfect for me
and my energy is exactly where it needs to be

I attract from my vibration that is here and now
I am so excited because I understand how

The choice is mine, it is my decision
I create what I want with clear thoughts and vision

I believe and allow—knowing without any doubt
that my thoughts do create what I send out

The frequency of my perfect other tunes in
and that "chance" meeting happens and it's time to begin

If it's not to my liking I must take a look at myself
shifting what's necessary to attract something else

—Mona McLaughlin

FREQUENCY FOUR: LOVE BOOSTERS

Release the Outcome

- Regularly practice a mind-body technique, such as yoga, tai chi, qi gong, etc.

- Align your energy by utilizing the services of a certified massage therapist, licensed acupuncturist, reiki, healing touch, or other healthcare professional.

- Make a list of *fun* things to do *without* a partner. Focus your attention on things that are rewarding to you. Do these things regularly.

- Create a "success list" of desirable things, people, or situations that you have previously manifested, such as a great friendship, new job, scholarship, etc. Remember how you felt when your desire came to fruition and savor the memory.

- Write your own fantasy love story with a very happy ending. Be sure to include a lot of juicy moments.

- Imagine sending your desires out into the Universe via a special messenger bird who will carry your invitation to the perfect person for you. A special meeting is being arranged for the two of you in the very near future—at the perfect time and place.

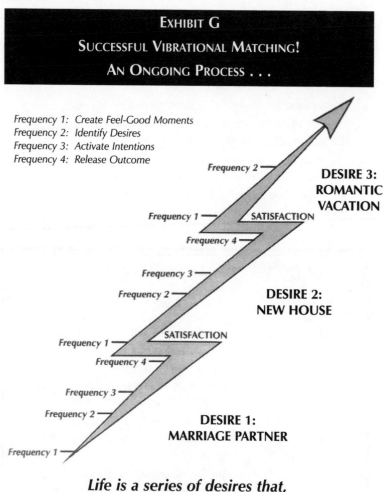

EXHIBIT G

SUCCESSFUL VIBRATIONAL MATCHING!

AN ONGOING PROCESS . . .

Frequency 1: Create Feel-Good Moments
Frequency 2: Identify Desires
Frequency 3: Activate Intentions
Frequency 4: Release Outcome

Frequency 2

DESIRE 3:
ROMANTIC
VACATION

Frequency 1 — SATISFACTION

Frequency 4

Frequency 3

Frequency 2 **DESIRE 2:**
NEW HOUSE

SATISFACTION
Frequency 1

Frequency 4

Frequency 3

Frequency 2 **DESIRE 1:**
MARRIAGE PARTNER

Frequency 1

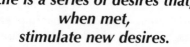

Life is a series of desires that,
when met,
stimulate new desires.

Kevin, with two delightful children, Linda is very grateful to the Universe that her wedding plans with Jay were canceled.

Releasing your wish to attract your highest good is the most positive action you can take. Go on, take the plunge; the water is incredibly inviting. You will discover that once you do, your life can flow with effortless ease and you can travel from one great adventure to another.

In either case, you can change your vibration by focusing your attention on what you desire—individuals who are emotionally available. Be aware of thoughts that are not in alignment with what you want to create, and practice shifting them in the direction of your desire. Set the intention to be a vibrational match for your desire, and you will become more conscious of when you are creating in the direction of what you do not want, rather than what you do want.

Can I avoid attracting guys who want me for my money by using Vibrational Matching?

—Desiring Integrity, Salt Lake City, Utah

Yes, Vibrational Matching works for creating all desires. It is important to focus your thoughts on what you want, and stop giving attention to your fears. Then you must align your thoughts, beliefs, and emotions in the direction of your desires. When we go out of our way to avoid things, we are in fact giving energy to whatever we are staying away from. Be aware of your emotions around any kind of avoidance and focus attention on your preferences.

I feel insecure about being overweight, but I would like to attract a slender woman. Is it possible to be a vibrational match to someone who is thin if you are not?

—Tired of Dieting, Austin, Texas

If you are comfortable with your weight, no matter what size you are, then you can attract your preference, whatever it may be. It is important for you to feel worthy in order for you to become a vibrational match to your desires. If you feel worthy, then you will increase your belief in your ability to create your desires, thus enhancing your attraction power.

Tune into Love

I am having an affair with my boss and I believe he is my "desirable vibrational match." Should I wait for him to leave his wife?

—Tired of Waiting, Madison, Wisconsin

When we focus on one particular person as being our desirable vibrational match, we place our peace of mind and happiness on hold, waiting for the relationship to come to fruition. This keeps our desires just beyond our reach.

Stay focused on your preferences, and the qualities of the person you desire rather than a particular individual. Remember to set the intention for the highest good for all concerned. If your boss is your desirable vibrational match, you will know in time. Relax and focus on your wholeness and well-being. It will work out perfectly no matter what the outcome.

I am happily married but my best friend is divorced and very lonely. Can I help him attract a girlfriend?

—John, Charlottesville, Virginia

Yes, you can help your friend by seeing him happy, whole, and relaxing into his well-being. Visualize him with a partner of his desires, if this is what he wants. As you hold this vision he will telepathically pick up on your positive vibrations, and it will support him to relax about his new single status. Feeling good about ourselves and our present life circumstances is important because we create new experiences from our current vibration.

I was feeling confident about attracting my ideal partner until the other day when my mother said she thought I shouldn't have such high expectations. I know she doesn't think I am very attractive or smart. What do I do now?

—Puzzled, Toronto, Canada

Hold your desires close to your heart. Do not make a practice of discussing your desires with others. Many people doubt their own ability to create their dreams, so they cannot support you in creating your desires. The only benefit of sharing your dreams is to feel supported, nurtured, and to exchange ideas with a loving friend or mentor. Share your dreams with only a select few if anyone at all, and be sure they have a track record for supporting you and offering unconditional love.

Is it better to stay focused on attracting one desire at a time?
—Single-Minded, Los Angeles, California

This is not necessary unless it feels more comfortable to you. The Universe can respond to multiple requests simultaneously. Have fun creating a Wish List for all of your desires, and watch your life unfold into one glorious moment after another.

How can I stay focused on what I want to create and at the same time release the outcome?
—Conflicted, Boulder, Colorado

Staying focused on what you want to create does not mean that you have to think about it all the time. It simply means that your thoughts are supportive and in alignment with your desires.

You can release the outcome by trusting in the process of the Law of Attraction, the abundance of the Universe, and knowing that if you have set the intention for your highest good, it will be forthcoming. It is through our personal experiences that we learn to trust in ourselves and in the process of co-creation. Begin by noticing your thoughts, beliefs, and feelings and correlating them with what you are attracting. You will see, in time, the validity of the process of co-creation.

Will my desirable vibrational match be for a lifetime?

—Marriage Wanted, Memphis, Tennessee

If you are a vibrational match for a lifetime mate, then, yes, it will be for a lifetime. If I were you, I would write this desire on my Wish List and line up my thoughts, beliefs, and feelings in the direction of creating a lifetime mate. The process of attracting a lifetime mate is the same as attracting any other preference you have listed on your Wish List.

Do I have to leave my current girlfriend to attract my desirable vibrational match?

—Holding on Tight, Jackson Hole, Wyoming

Why would you want to continue dating someone who is not your desirable vibrational match? Your question implies that you do not trust that you can have it all. Is your current girlfriend a security blanket so you will have someone to be with in case your desirable vibrational match does not show up? Are you staying in the relationship because you are afraid of being alone? If so, you may be keeping your dreams just outside your reach.

Your question indicates that you are fearful both of being alone and of not having what you really desire. It is possible to experience fear and yet consciously take steps to overcome it, moving up the vibrational ladder in the direction of your desires. However, if you allow fear to keep you from taking risks, then it becomes an inhibitor to you becoming a vibrational match for your desires.

My wife died six months ago and I want to find someone, but I feel guilty about dating so soon. How can I attract my desirable vibrational match?

—Ready to Take a Chance Again, Omaha, Nebraska

Guilt is resistance, and it inhibits us from being a vibrational match to our desires because, like any negative emotion, it lowers our frequency level. You can release guilt by setting the intention to feel comfortable about creating a new relationship. Allow the Universe to inspire you to thoughts that will help you create a new perspective on dating. Consciously and gently, step by step, you will shift your thoughts in the direction of your new desire.

My spiritual beliefs are aligned with being vegetarian. However, I have not been able to attract a vegetarian man into my life. Everything else on my Wish List is fulfilled but this one keeps getting missed. What's the deal here?
—ISO Animal Lover, Baltimore, Maryland

If you have negative thoughts about a non-vegetarian lifestyle, then you will attract men who are non-vegetarians into your experience. Our negative thoughts hold us to what we resist, causing us to attract exactly what we are fighting against. Be guided by the Law of Allowing and accept the choices made by others even when those choices are different from your own personal preferences. By doing this you will raise your vibration and open yourself up to attracting your desires.

I know I can control my conscious thoughts in creating my desirable vibrational match, but how can I control my unconscious thoughts?
—Mind-boggled, San Diego, California

Focus on your conscious thoughts and do not be concerned about your unconscious thoughts. Set intentions for what you want, and keep your thoughts pointed in the direction of your desires by monitoring your emotions. By setting clear, strong intentions, your unconscious thoughts will come into alignment with your desires.

Tune into Love

I want to leave my boyfriend but he depends on me for emotional and financial support. I really care about him as a friend, but I know he is not the "right" guy for me. He is on antidepressants and may become more depressed if I leave him. How can I depart and still be a good friend?
—Fearful, Arlington, Virginia

Integrity is always the answer. Are you coming from a place of integrity if you stay in a relationship that is not right for you? Of course not! You must follow your heart and trust that the Universe will support both of you through this decision. Set the intention for the highest good for all concerned and allow yourself to be guided in how and when to leave the relationship. If your partner is not the "right" one for you, then you can be sure that you are not the "right" one for him. He deserves to be with someone who can love him as a partner. Staying in a relationship because of fear is not in anyone's best interest. See him from a higher place and know that he can "make it" on his own. By sending positive thoughts into the Universe you will support him in raising his vibration, which is the mark of a true friend.

Frequently Asked Questions

Oh softly touch
Your spirit be
In dreams not held
For other see

Oh give within
As give without
In dreams that hold
To moments doubt

As reach you must
Cascading through
The dreams you hold
In moments true

For spirits born
In visions see
Lead now to love
To moments be

—Jim Burns

Epilogue

A Vibrational Matching Book for Couples will be coming soon. Look for:

Tune into Your Love

It is only a matter of time before you become a vibrational match to your desires. Once you have attracted the relationship of your dreams, it will be valuable for you to learn vibrational and other therapeutic techniques to build a loving and lasting partnership.

Some people believe you cannot continue your psychological or spiritual growth unless you are married. They believe that you must be legally bound to another person in order to be willing to "stick it out" and work through challenges.

I firmly believe that tremendous growth can occur in all stages of intimate relationships. People grow because they are willing, have the tools, and are committed to doing so, not because of an obligation.

Vibrational Matching techniques integrated with therapeutic modalities provide willing participants the tools to inspire growth. Inspiration is a much happier way to learn life's lessons and affirm our wholeness.

I look forward to helping you create and enhance the relationship of your dreams as we move into phase two, *Tune into Your Love.*

Endnotes

Introduction
1. Joseph Campbell, ed. *The Portable Jung*, p. 505.

Chapter One
1. Harville Hendrix, Ph.D., *Getting the Love You Want*, p. 49.
2. Ibid.
3. Dean Radin, Ph.D., *The Conscious Universe*, pp. 6, 13, 281.
4. Ibid., pp. 6, 281.
5. Ibid., p. 226.
6. Ibid., p. 227.
7. Ibid., p. 290.
8. Ibid., pp. 79, 88.
9. Jessica Utts, "An Assessment of the Evidence for Psychic Functioning," *Journal of Scientific Exploration,* vol. 10, no. 1, 1996, pp. 3–30. Ray Hyman, "Evaluation of a Program on Anomalous Mental Phenomena," *Journal of Scientific Exploration*, vol. 10, no. 1, 1996, pp. 31–58.
10. Russell Targ, *Limitless Mind*, p. 107.
11. Radin, *The Conscious Universe*, p. 114.
12. Dean I. Radin and R. D. Nelson, "Evidence for Consciousness-Related Anomalies in Random Physical Systems," *Foundations of Physics Journal,* December,1989.
13. Larry Dossey, M.D., *Healing Words*, p. 242.
14. Targ, *Limitless Mind*, p. 148.

15. W. G. Braud, G. Davis, and R. Wood, "Experiments with Matthew Manning," *Journal of the American Society for Psychical Research,* vol. 50, no. 782, 1979, pp. 199–223.

16. William G. Braud, "Distant Mental Influence of Rate of Hemolysis of Human Red Blood Cells," *Journal of the American Society for Psychical Research* 84, no. 1, January 1990, pp. 1–24.

17. Howard Wolinsky, "Prayers Do Aid Sick, Study Finds," *Chicago Sun-Times,* January 26, 1986, p. 30. Byrd's original study is published in Randolph C. Byrd, "Positive Therapeutic Effects of Intercessory Prayer in a Coronary Care Unit Population," *Southern Medical Journal* 81:7, July 1988, pp. 826–29.

18. Daniel J. Benor, "Survey of Spiritual Healing Research," *Complementary Medical Research* 4, no. 1, September 1990, pp. 9–33.

19. Radin, *The Conscious Universe,* pp. 172–174.

20. Michael Schmicker, *Best Evidence,* NE, Writer's Club Press, 2000, p. 179. http://www.sprintweb.org/Sprint/obe-faq.html.

21. Lynne McTaggart, *The Field,* p. 138.

22. Radin, *The Conscious Universe,* p. 15.

23. G. Schwartz, et al., "Accuracy and Replicability of Anomalous After-Death Communication Across Highly Skilled Mediums," *Journal of the Society for Psychical Research,* vol. 65.1, no. 862, 2001, pp. 1–25.

24. Targ, *Limitless Mind,* p. 102.

25. C. G. Jung, *Synchronicity: An Acausal Connecting Principle,* p. 81.

26. Ibid.

27. Radin, *The Conscious Universe,* p. 173.

Chapter 3

1. Phillip Wayne (trans.), *Faust, Part Two,* p. 79.

Glossary

ALLOWER: A person who understands and lives by the Law of Allowing is called an allower. An allower accepts himself and/or others attracting undesirable experiences without judging, worrying, or putting other negative thoughts around himself or others. An allower feels love and compassion for himself and for all others.

CO-CREATE: Allowing the vibration of others to influence what you create.

CO-CREATION IN YOUR HIGHEST GOOD: Allowing the pure vibration of consciousness to inspire and guide us so we can transcend the perceived limitations of the physical world and create synchronistic events. When we focus on desires, co-creation gives us access to the entire Universe.

COLLECTIVE CONSCIOUSNESS: An ocean of thoughts, beliefs, and emotions of every living thing in the Universe that when accessed, can guide and inspire us.

DELIBERATE CREATION: The process of aligning thoughts, beliefs, and emotion with desires.

DOMINANT VIBRATION: Magnetizes our experiences, and is determined by the combined frequency of our thoughts, beliefs, and feelings regarding a particular desire.

EMOTIONAL GUIDANCE SYSTEM: Provides clarity to us with regard to the direction of our thoughts. When our emotions are positive, our thoughts are in alignment with our desires. When our emotions are negative, our thoughts are not in alignment with our desires.

EMOTIONS: Create a vibration that moves our thoughts and desires throughout the Universe. The stronger the emotion, the more powerful the movement is through space and time.

ENERGIZE: To attrace someone or something through your vibrational frequency. When you energize something you are sending thoughts into the Universe that are in alignment with your vibration.

FEELING TONE: The level of intensity of the passion associated with a particular desire, which can be positive or negative.

FREQUENCY: The rate of movement of energy in wave formations is known as frequency.

INTENTION: Blending strong desire with strong belief to create a deliberate outcome.

INTUITION: Intuition is a type of psychic phenomenon. It expresses itself through our senses and can be received in various ways including telepathy, clairvoyance, clairaudience, precognition, or field consciousness.

KINESIOLOGY: The study of muscles, used to calibrate consciousness.

LAW OF ALLOWING: Freedom from negativity; releasing resistance to the choices made by you or others; releasing resistance to what you or others have attracted; absence of judgment of self or others; the process of allowing creates positive emotion; it is different from tolerating, which is "putting up with" something that displeases you. Tolerating creates negative emotion while allowing creates positive emotion.

Glossary

LAW OF ATTRACTION: The basis in which the entire Universe operates. The Law of Attraction can be defined as: vibrations of similar frequencies are magnetized to each other. In essence, thought draws in other thoughts of a similar vibration.

MAGNETIC ATTRACTION: The dominant vibrational frequencies of two individuals are in resonance. The stronger the resonance between two people, the stronger will be the chemistry or magnetic attraction.

RESONANCE: Two frequencies attuned to each other.

ROMANTIC CHEMISTRY: Occurs when the dominant vibrational frequencies of two individuals are in resonance. It occurs because a magnetic attraction between two people exists.

UNIVERSE: This is a higher power that is the pure source of all energy, infinite intelligence that is available to all of us.

VIBRATIONAL MATCHING: Is the deliberate intention to attract our desires—in this case, a romantic relationship—by aligning and focusing our thoughts, emotions, and beliefs with what we want.

VIBRATIONAL SYNCHRONICITY: Alignment of frequencies in such a way that a meaningful coincidence of two or more events occurs, where something other than the probability of chance is involved.

VIBRATIONS: Movement of energy in wave formations. Individuals are perceived by the Universe as a vibration. Your thoughts, beliefs, and emotions make up your consciousness, which is interpreted by everything in the Universe as energy.

Bibliography

Baumann, T. Lee, M.D. *God at the Speed of Light: The Melding of Science and Spirituality*. Virginia Beach, Va.: A.R.E. Press, 2002.

Beaulieu, John. *Music and Sound in the Healing Arts*. Barrytown, N.Y.: Station Hill Press, 1987.

Bohm, David. *Wholeness and the Implicate Order*. London; Boston: Routledge & Kegan Paul, 1980.

———. *Quantum Theory*. New York: Dover Publications, 1989.

Campbell, Don. *Music and Miracles*. Wheaton, Ill.: Quest Books, 1992.

———. *The Mozart Effect*. New York: HarperCollins, 2001.

Campbell, Joseph, ed. *The Portable Jung*. New York: Viking Press, 1971.

Capra, Fritjof. *The Turning Point: Science, Society, and the Rising Culture*. New York: Bantam Books, 1983.

———. *The Tao of Physics*. Boston, Mass.: Shambhala, 1991.

———. *The Hidden Connections: Integrating the Biological, Cognitive, and Social Dimensions of Life into a Science of Sustainability*. New York: Doubleday, 2002.

Cerutti, Edwina. *Olga Worrall: Mystic with the Healing Hands*. San Francisco: Harper and Row, 1975.

Cohen, Alan. *I Had It All the Time*. Carlsbad, Calif.: Hay House, 1995.

———. *A Deep Breath of Life*. Carlsbad, Calif.: Hay House, 1996.

Cohen, Alan H. *Why Your Life Sucks . . . and What You Can Do About It*. San Diego: Jodere Group, 2002.

Dewhurst-Maddock, Olivea. *The Book of Sound Therapy*. New York: Simon & Schuster, 1993.

Dossey, Larry, M.D. *Recovering the Soul: A Scientific and Spiritual Search*. New York: Bantam Books, 1989.

———. *Healing Words: The Power of Prayer and the Practice of Medicine*. San Francisco: HarperSanFrancisco, 1993.

Dyer, Wayne W., Ph.D. *The Power of Intention*. Carlsbad, Calif.: Hay House, 2004.

Emoto, Masaru. *The Hidden Messages in Water*. Hillsboro, Ore.: Beyond Words, 2004.

Feldman, Jane Howard. *Commune with the Angels*. Virginia Beach, Va.: A.R.E. Press, 1992.

Gerber, Richard, M.D. *Vibrational Medicine*. Rochester, Vt.: Bear and Company, 2001.

Goldman, Jonathan. *Healing Sounds: The Power of Harmonics*. Rockport, Mass.: Element Books, 1992.

———. *Shifting Frequencies*. Flagstaff, Ariz.: Light Technology, 1998.

Hawkins, David R., M.D., Ph.D. *Power vs. Force: The Hidden Determinants of Human Behavior*. Carlsbad, Calif.: Hay House, 2002.

Hendrix, Harville. *Getting the Love You Want: A Guide for Couples*. New York: Henry Holt and Company, 1988.

Hicks, Esther and Jerry. *Ask and It Is Given: Learning to Manifest Your Desires*. Carlsbad, Calif.: Hay House, 2004.

Hicks, Jerry and Esther. *A New Beginning I: Handbook for Joyous Survival*. San Antonio, Tex.: Abraham-Hicks Publications, 1996.

———. *A New Beginning II: A Personal Handbook to Enhance Your Life, Liberty and Pursuit of Happiness*. San Antonio, Tex.: Abraham-Hicks Publications, 1996.

Jacobi, Jolande. *The Psychology of C. G. Jung*. New Haven, Conn.: Yale University Press, 1973.

Jones, Roger S. *Physics for the Rest of Us*. Chicago: Contemporary Books, 1992.

Jung, C. G. *Modern Man in Search of a Soul*. London: Kegan Paul, Trench, Trubler & Co., 1933.

———. *The Archetypes and the Collective Unconscious*. Princeton, N.J.: Princeton University Press, 1959.

———. *Aion: Researches into the Phenomenology of the Self*. Princeton, N.J.: Princeton University Press, 1969.

———. *Synchronicity: An Acausal Connecting Principle*. Princeton: Princeton University Press, 1973.

———. *Psychology and the Occult*. Princeton, N.J.: Princeton University Press, 1977.

Bibliography

Long, Max Freedom. *Recovering the Ancient Magic*. Cape Girardeau, Mo.: Huna Press, 1978.

McTaggart, Lynne. *The Field: The Quest for the Secret Force of the Universe*. New York: HarperCollins, 2002.

Orloff, Judith, M.D. *Second Sight*. New York: Warner Books, 1996.

Radin, Dean, Ph.D. *The Conscious Universe*. New York: HarperEdge, 1997.

Riggle, Jon, Joe Preller, and Mike Breschi. *Dating with Success*. Baltimore, Md.: J.M.J. Publications, 1995.

Rosenberg, Larry and David Guy. *Breath by Breath: The Liberating Practice of Insight Meditation*. Boston, Mass.: Shambhala, 1998.

Schroeder, Gerald L. *The Hidden Face of God: Science Reveals the Ultimate Truth*. New York: Free Press, 2001.

Seligman, Martin E. P., Ph.D. *Learned Optimism: How to Change Your Mind and Your Life*. New York: Pocket Books, 1991.

Shamdasani, Sonu. *Jung and the Making of Modern Psychology: The Dream of a Science*. Cambridge, UK: Cambridge University Press, 2003.

Silva, Jose, and Philip Miele. *The Silva Mind Control Method*. New York: Simon & Schuster, 1977.

Stevens, Anthony. *Jung: A Very Short Introduction*. New York: Oxford University Press, 2001.

Talbot, Michael. *The Holographic Universe*. New York: Perennial, 1992.

Targ, Russell. *Limitless Mind*. Novato, Calif.: New World Library, 2004.

Tiller, William A., Ph.D. *Science and Human Transformation: Subtle Energies, Intentionality and Consciousness*. Walnut Creek, Calif.: Pavior, 1997.

Tipler, Frank J. *The Physics of Immortality*. New York: Anchor Books, 1995.

Walsch, Neale Donald. *Conversations with God: An Uncommon Dialogue*. 3 vols. Charlottesville, Va.: Hampton Roads, 1995–1998.

Wayne, Phillip (trans.). *Faust, Part Two*. Harmondsworth, England: Penguin Books Ltd., 1959.

Weiss, Brian L., M.D. *Many Lives, Many Masters*. New York: Fireside, 1988.

White, Stewart Edward. *The Unobstructed Universe*. Columbus, Ohio: Ariel Press, 1988.

Worrall, Ambrose A., and Olga Worrall. *The Gift of Healing: A Personal Story of Spiritual Therapy*. Columbus, Ohio: Ariel Press, 1985.

———. *Explore Your Psychic World*. Columbus, Ohio: Ariel Press, 1989.

About the Author

A licensed psychotherapist and motivational speaker, Margaret McCraw, Ph.D., lives, as well as teaches, the principles she presents in *Tune into Love.* As founder and president of The Institute of Vibrational Synchronicity, she provides personal as well as executive coaching and training to a wide variety of organizations and professionals. In addition, as a faculty member of the American Holistic University, Margaret teaches in the doctoral program for Transpersonal Counseling Psychology.

With more than 25 years of experience as a healthcare and business consultant, she works with psychologists, marriage/ relationship therapists, nurses, social workers, mental health counselors, and life coaches. Her seminars focus on raising one's level of vibration, enabling individuals, couples, and organizations to achieve their desires. An inspiring speaker, she travels nationwide, sharing her insights on personal empowerment, manifesting one's dreams, relationship building, and business development.

Margaret McCraw has seen miracles become an everyday reality after clients begin practicing vibration techniques. It was these experiences that inspired her to write this book.

The Institute of Vibrational Synchronicity

Call toll free, 1-877-366-9111, or visit Margaret McCraw's web site at www.margaretmccraw.com for information on counseling and training services.

The institute offers the following programs:

VIBRATIONAL SYNCHRONICITY COUNSELING

Vibrational Synchronicity counseling is provided in person or over the telephone depending upon your location and the availability of a certified counselor. Counselors have completed the certification program for psychotherapists and life coaches. Counseling services are based on integrating vibrational techniques with other therapeutic and life enhancement skills to help you create your dreams.

VIBRATIONAL SYNCHRONICITY WORKSHOPS FOR THE GENERAL PUBLIC

These workshops are intended to teach participants vibrational principles and tools combined with other life enhancement skills, deepening the participant's understanding of how to create a fulfilling life. In addition to lectures there are experiential sessions, exercises, and a group discussion led by the facilitator.

THE VIBRATIONAL SYNCHRONICITY CERTIFICATION PROGRAM FOR PSYCHOTHERAPISTS, LIFE COACHES, AND OTHER HEALTHCARE PROFESSIONALS

These workshops are for professionals who work with clients in a counseling, coaching, or healing capacity. The interactive group sessions are focused on integrating vibrational techniques with other clinical and therapeutic modalities. Continuing education units ("CEU") are available for some professionals.

THE VIBRATIONAL SYNCHRONICITY CERTIFICATION PROGRAM FOR ORGANIZATIONAL LEADERSHIP

There are three levels in which organizations can invest in the Leadership Program. These interactive group sessions are focused on integrating vibrational techniques with other business strategies. Continuing education units ("CEU") are available for some professionals.

1. Executive Forum—This program is for senior executives and board members who desire to understand how to use vibrational techniques combined with leadership skills, quality improvement, and other business strategies to achieve their organizational vision and enhance their overall bottom line.
2. Management Forum—This program is for middle managers and supervisory personnel. It focuses on teaching managers how to achieve departmental goals by using vibrational techniques combined with supervisory skills, quality improvement, and other business strategies.
3. Employee Forum—This program is for front-line staff. It teaches employees vibrational techniques combined with

quality improvement enhancements, and other business strategies to increase overall performance, including productivity, efficiency, and effectiveness.

MANDALA INFORMATION

For information regarding ordering mandalas and mandala interpretations please go to Margaret McCraw's web site: www.margaretmccraw.com.

Hampton Roads Publishing Company

. . . for the evolving human spirit

HAMPTON ROADS PUBLISHING COMPANY publishes books on a variety of subjects, including metaphysics, spirituality, health, visionary fiction, and other related topics.

We also create on-line courses and sponsor an *Applied Learning Series* of author workshops. For a current list of what is available, go to www.hrpub.com or request the ALS workshop catalog at our toll-free number.

For a copy of our latest trade catalog or consumer catalog, call toll-free, 800-766-8009, or send your name and address to:

HAMPTON ROADS PUBLISHING COMPANY, INC.
1125 STONEY RIDGE ROAD · CHARLOTTESVILLE, VA 22902
e-mail: hrpc@hrpub.com · www.hrpub.com